I0458814

Unsealed Diaries of Married and Divorced Couples

Confessions, Regrets, and Affairs -The Messy Truth About

Love, Lies, and Who Really Left the Toilet Seat Up

Nicole Levington
&
Ted Shubbard

Unsealed Diaries of Married and Divorced Couples

Confessions, Regrets, and Affairs -The Messy Truth About

Love, Lies, and Who Really Left the Toilet Seat Up

Copyright©2025

All rights reserved by Nicole Levington & Ted Shubbard

Published in the United States by Cross Border Publishers.

No part of this publication may be reproduced, stored, or transmitted in any form or by any means electronic, mechanical, photocopying, recording, or otherwise without prior written permission from the author or publisher, except for brief excerpts used in reviews or educational purposes as permitted by law.

This book is protected under U.S. and international copyright laws. Unauthorized reproduction, distribution, or adaptation of any portion of this work may result in legal consequences.

For permissions, licensing, or inquiries, please contact

info@crossborderpublishers.com: www.crossborderpublishers.com

Book Formatting by: Monisha

Book cover design by: *Billy Design*

CROSSBORDER

New York, London, Quebec

Contents

Introduction

Welcome to the laboratory of human romantic dysfunction, where love comes with disclaimers and relationships arrive with assembly instructions that nobody reads until something breaks. This collection of confessions, statistical oddities, and uncomfortable truths serves as your field guide to the beautiful disaster we call modern romance.

Come ride with us as we discover that 73% of people have lied about their cooking abilities on dating apps, that the average couple argues about toilet seat positioning 2.3 times per month, and that "working late" has become the Swiss Army knife of marital deception. Ever wonder why wedding planners keep therapists on speed dial, how GPS tracking has revolutionized both navigation and paranoia, and the exact moment when "I love you" transforms from declaration to negotiation tactic?

The data doesn't lie—even when we do. Research reveals patterns more twisted than earphone cables left in pockets. Married couples spend an average of fourteen minutes daily discussing whose turn it is to take out the trash, yet only three minutes actually taking it out. Dating app users swipe through potential soulmates faster than they scroll through takeout menus, and 89% of people claim they want honesty in relationships while simultaneously googling "how to delete browser history."

From the archaeology of abandoned wedding rings found in Uber seats to the anthropology of passive-aggressive Post-it note warfare, these pages chronicle humanity's most persistent hobby: making love complicated. Each fact has been carefully curated from the wreckage of real relationships, complete with statistical proof that we're all magnificently, consistently, and hilariously human in our romantic endeavors.

Prepare to laugh, cringe, and possibly recognize yourself in these revelations. After all, misery loves company, but comedy loves an audience.

Thank you in advance for reading. Ted and I (Nicole) promise you a great time ahead.

Chapter 1

The Fairy-Tale Hangover – When Love Meets Reality

The Fairy-Tale Hangover – When Love Meets Reality

Once upon a time, every love story ended with a magical "happily ever after". The curtains fell as our fairy-tale couple rode off into the sunset, leaving us with warm fuzzies and the unquestioned notion that love conquers all. Then real life happened. The next morning, Prince Charming's socks were on the floor, Cinderella had morning breath, and nobody wanted to do the dishes. Welcome to the fairy-tale hangover: when love meets reality. It's that sobering (and often hilarious) moment we realize that real romance has less to do with glass slippers and more to do with garbage disposals. In this chapter, we'll navigate four unglamorous truths about modern love – with a wink and a laugh – to see how *ever after* is less about magic carpets and more about laundry piles and credit scores.

Rom-Com vs. Reality: Grand Gestures and Dirty Dishes

We've all seen those rom-com moments: the grand airport chase, where the hero races through security to profess his love before the heroine's plane takes off, or the rain-soaked kiss that miraculously looks gorgeous instead of giving both actors pneumonia. On-screen, love is a highlight reel of choreographed gestures – think *Say Anything*'s boombox serenade or *The Notebook*'s passionate downpour kiss – all set to a swelling soundtrack. But real life love? Let's just say the soundtrack is more likely the sloshing of dishwater and the drone of a laundry machine. When your partner chases you down in real life, it's probably to hand you the trash bag you forgot to put out, not a bouquet of roses at the airport. Try reenacting a movie-style last-minute airport declaration today and you'll likely end up on a no-fly list rather than in someone's arms (airport security doesn't appreciate a rom-com moment). And that iconic cinematic kiss in the pouring rain? In reality, you'd both be shivering, soggy, and arguing about who left the umbrella at home.

In Hollywood, nobody ever seems to wash a dish or scrub a toilet. Yet in the real world, love often blooms in the grocery aisle and the laundry room. The unsung romance of everyday coupledom is in those little un-cinematic chores: folding each other's underwear, teaming up to hunt down a mysterious odor in the fridge, or celebrating a Friday night by finally tackling that mountainous pile of laundry. Sharing these daily tasks might not be movie montage material, but it turns out they're crucial to real relationship happiness. Surveys confirm what your grandmother could have told you: nearly *80% of couples* admit they have disagreements about household chores. (The other 20% either have a cleaning service or a fairy godmother on retainer.) Hollywood may give us grand gestures, but actual couples are over here bickering about dishwasher loading techniques and whose turn it is to take out the recycling. In fact, research suggests that figuring out how to stack the dishwasher together can be an oddly profound bonding experience – couples who coordinate on chores often develop better communication and a stronger sense of fairness in the relationship. Who knew that loading cutlery and debating proper plate placement could be a form of foreplay for communication skills?

The contrast between rom-com romance and reality can be downright comic. In movies, a passionate lover might stand outside your window with cue cards (*Love Actually*-style) or break into a spontaneous dance number in the street. In real life, romance is your partner braving Costco on a Saturday or waking up early to walk the dog when it's your turn. Real romance hides in life's mundanities. As one humor writer wryly notes, sharing Netflix passwords and splitting the chore list is a lot more useful to long-term love than megaphone serenades. Candlelit dinners and kissing in the rain are great, but have you ever had someone remember your convoluted coffee order *and* unclog the sink before you got home? Swoon. Indeed, modern love often means appreciating the small, unglamorous acts of care. A partner who will patiently untangle the hair clog from the shower drain is arguably demonstrating more devotion than one who hires a plane to skywrite "I love you" (and is certainly being more helpful around the house).

Romantic comedies also never prepare us for how *persistent* the boring stuff is. Montage scenes might show one cute bubble bath or a single bout of painting a new apartment, but they skip over the fifth time this week you're debating how to load the washing machine. And yet, these very moments can be strangely intimate. There's a quiet comedy and comfort in the routine: two people in mismatched pajamas brushing their teeth side by side (spitting toothpaste, not exactly cinematic!), or high-fiving because you finally fixed that wobbly cabinet door together. Real love is less about one-time grand gestures and more about everyday teamwork. In fact, couples who share mundane tasks tend to be happier and even report higher relationship satisfaction (and yes, a better sex life) than those who don't. One Cornell study found that couples who split household chores fairly had more "action in the bedroom" as a bonus. Who would've thought that doing the dishes and taking out the trash could be an aphrodisiac? It seems scrubbing the skillet together might beat a rose-petal bath for keeping the spark alive. So the next time you're feeling bad that your love life isn't like the movies, remember: sharing a pizza on the couch while folding laundry can be just as romantic, in its own wonderfully ordinary way. In the rom-com of real life, the grand finale isn't an airport kiss — it's two people collapsed on the couch, exhausted from cleaning the house, smiling at each other because the chores are done *and* you're in it together.

In fairy tales, when Cinderella marries Prince Charming, nobody asks if the Prince has student loans or how he handles his credit card bills. Fast forward to the 21st century, and modern dating involves a lot more than a glass slipper — try credit scores, budgets, and background checks. Today, Prince Charming might need a charming FICO score to match. You could be the most ardent romantic, but it's hard to plan a happily ever after without also planning who's going to pay the electric bill. Real-life love means gazing into each other's eyes… and eventually discussing the grim reality of joint checking accounts and the APR on your car loan. Forget slaying dragons; contemporary couples are teaming up to slay debt and tame the monthly budget spreadsheets. As unsexy as it sounds, many a modern relationship milestone comes when you both sit down, possibly with a bottle of wine for courage, to share your financial skeletons: "I owe how much on my student loans, dear?" *clutching pearls*, "And you have how many unpaid parking tickets?"

If that doesn't sound romantic, you're not alone – but it is reality. Consider this: 87% of soon-to-be married couples share their credit scores with each other, and a whopping 83% have come clean about all their outstanding debt. In other words, the new "what's your sign?" might be "what's your credit score?" (And perhaps, "are we financially compatible?") Dating apps won't put it in your profile, but maybe they should – because money matters can make or break the fairy tale. Surveys consistently find that money is one of the top conflict triggers for couples. Nearly half of partners – about *45%* – admit to arguing about money at least occasionally, and roughly one in four couples says money issues are the greatest relationship challenge of all. It's almost poetic justice: for all the emphasis on love and passion, it's the bills and the budgeting that often cause the most drama. (Who needs a wicked stepmother stirring up trouble when you have a $300 cable bill to argue over?)

The collision of love and money leads to some absurd and awkward moments that rom-coms never prepare us for. Picture a candlelit dinner where, instead of sweet nothings, you're whispering about whether to file taxes jointly or separately. Or that sexy night in that turns into a spreadsheet review of your monthly expenses. There's dark comedy in two lovers sitting on the couch, surrounded by takeout containers, muttering *"Did you really spend $200 on pop-culture figurines this month?"* and

"We need to talk about our data plan overage." Perhaps that's why financial transparency has become a core part of modern relationships – couples know that love won't pay the rent (not unless your landlord accepts kisses and IOUs). Many even take proactive steps: almost 1 in 5 couples have postponed their wedding to save more money for it, which is something no fairy tale ever mentioned (Sleeping Beauty didn't wake up and say "Prince, let's delay the castle wedding until we're financially stable," but welcome to reality). And if you do go through with the dream wedding? Well, about 40% of newlyweds are still busy paying off that wedding debt in the first year of marriage – the party may be over, but the credit card bills are the gift that keeps on giving.

One of the funniest (and slightly horrifying) realities of modern love is the specter of student loan debt. Fairy tales never warned us that finding "the one" might also mean inheriting $1.77 trillion in national student debt burden, collectively speaking. Yes, Americans owe nearly *1.8 trillion dollars* in student loans as of 2025, which is a decidedly un-enchanting number. Instead of a fairy-tale kingdom, many young couples are bringing two sets of student loans into the relationship and tying the knot *and* their debt loads together. Imagine Cinderella discovering Prince Charming's castle is mortgaged to the hilt, or that he's still paying off his sword-fighting academy tuition. In today's terms, that's not far off: marriage sometimes means marrying each other's debts – "for richer or poorer" has never been more literal. In fact, three in five Americans say they've considered postponing or avoiding marriage to not take on a partner's debt. While the prospect of eternal love is wonderful, eternal loan payments are not exactly the stuff of romance. It can be a mood-killer to discuss whose student loans have the higher interest rate or who's responsible for what portion of the mortgage, but modern couples find ways to laugh through it. ("Roses are red, violets are blue, our credit score's 682 – that okay with you?")

The practical aspects of love don't end at debts and bills. There's also the ongoing saga of budgeting and spending styles. You might be soulmates, but are you budget-mates? Is one of you a saver and the other a spender? Cue the sitcom scenarios: one partner brings home a new gadget or a pair of expensive shoes and the other raises an eyebrow like, "Really, was this in the budget?" Money habits can be as ingrained (and incompatible) as royal lineage in a fairy tale. It's no surprise that financial "infidelity" – hiding purchases or secret stashes of money – is a thing now, with around 22% of newlyweds admitting they keep some financial secrets from their spouse. Who needs an affair when you can sneak-buy pricey Starbucks lattes and stash the evidence? Modern love sometimes involves discovering an Amazon package on the doorstep and demanding, in mock outrage, "Honey, what did you order this time?"

And let's not forget the unromantic but necessary conversations about future planning: insurance policies, retirement funds, maybe even prenuptial agreements. Bringing up a prenup over a candlelit dinner is the dating equivalent of a record scratch – and yet about 15% of couples do consider prenups before marriage, and a much larger percentage end up signing some form of marital agreement once reality sets in. It's not that romance dies in these conversations; it's that romance has to scoot over and make room for realism. Couples learn to navigate these talks with humor and honesty. You might joke about it: *"Nothing says I love you like running a free credit report on each other,"* or *"Our love is eternal, but just in case it's not, here's a legal document."* Indeed, Prince Charming's credit score has become as relevant as his charm. Far from undermining love, tackling these issues together can *strengthen* a relationship – it's you two against the world (and its bills), a united front to achieve that happily ever after (with a balanced checkbook).

So yes, the castle of contemporary love has a few more rooms to clean – the budget room, the debt dungeon, the cupboard of monthly bills – but navigating them can bring couples closer in ways the fairy tales never showed. There's a strange kind of romance in forging a life together in practical terms. When you and your partner conquer a credit card payoff or celebrate hitting a savings goal, it's a victory for Team Love. It may not be the stuff of storybooks, but it's deeply satisfying. After all, anyone can share a champagne toast on a rooftop; it takes real partnership to share a Netflix account and a joint savings plan without killing each other. As absurd as it sounds, discussing health insurance options or whose name the car title should be in can actually bolster intimacy – it means you're building a real life together, not just a fantasy. And if you can find humor in the process (laughing through the tax prep or doing silly voices while reading the fine print on a mortgage), you're basically invincible. Modern love demands pragmatism, but it doesn't preclude passion – it just means passion might occasionally wear a suit and tie and bring a calculator to date night.

"You Complete Me" (And Other Lies We Love)

When Jerry Maguire famously told Dorothy "You complete me," audiences everywhere swooned into their popcorn. It was the ultimate romantic line – the idea that we are incomplete halves waiting for that perfect other half to make us whole. Cue the collective *awww*. But step away from the Hollywood glow, and that line starts to look less like a dream and more like a dubious relationship strategy. Do we really want to be incomplete halves? In theory, it sounds poetic; in practice, it's a lot of pressure to put on someone to be your everything (not to mention a fast track to losing yourself). As one relationship expert dryly noted, *the idea that someone else should "complete" you is a giant red flag and often a recipe for partnership failure.* Healthy love, they tell us, is not about two half-formed souls merging into a single entity; it's about two whole (and sometimes wonderfully messy) people choosing to share a life. In other words, real relationships are less "you complete me" and more "we complement each other, but darn if we don't still have to assemble this IKEA bookcase together."

And oh, the IKEA bookcase. If there is any event that exposes the fallacy of "you complete me," it's a couple's attempt to assemble flat-pack furniture. Few things test the limits of love like a do-it-yourself shelving unit with vague instructions and too many screws. One might even say IKEA is the modern couple's crucible. Therapists have joked (only half-seriously) that a trip to IKEA is like a relationship stress test, a maze of decisions and teamwork trials that can reveal communication breakdowns faster than you can say "Allen wrench." In fact, so many couples report fighting while shopping for or assembling IKEA furniture that some counselors literally use it as a diagnostic exercise. One Wall Street Journal report described a therapist who asks feuding partners to assemble a piece of IKEA furniture together and observes what happens. It's therapy, Scandinavian style. There's even an infamous item – the daunting Liatorp wall unit – nicknamed *"the Divorcemaker"* because of its legendary difficulty and the arguments it sparks. (Imagine two otherwise sane people hurling tiny wooden dowels at each other in despair. True love, folks.) Surveys find that 17% of couples get into an argument every single time they attempt to assemble furniture together. If "you complete me" were true, wouldn't assembling a simple bookshelf be a breeze since you two are perfectly meshed? Ha! Instead, what usually happens is more like: one person insists they're reading the instructions right while the other person swears the instructions must be wrong, and an hour later nobody is speaking except to accuse the other of hiding part B or screwing part C in backwards.

The beauty (and comedy) of real relationships is that they involve two independent people colliding in all their wholeness and quirks. Rather than fixing each other or fitting together like puzzle pieces, couples often find themselves more like two adjacent tornadoes occasionally bumping into one another's path of chaos. And that's okay! Real love isn't about solving all your partner's problems or filling all their voids – it's about witnessing each other's full selves (voids, rough edges and all) and still saying, "I'm here for it." It's two *whole* people who sometimes make an absolute mess together: literally (see aforementioned IKEA showdown or the flour explosion from attempting to bake brownies as a duo) and figuratively. If you enter a relationship feeling like a fractional half-person searching for your other half, you might end up more lost than found. As psychologist Deborah Hecker points out, depending on another person for your sense of completion is unhealthy; each person needs to maintain their own identity and wholeness. Or put more bluntly: *"The idea that someone should complete you is central to the failure of partnerships."* Ouch. Sorry, Jerry Maguire. In reality, a great relationship is not two halves becoming one, but two ones forming a "we" – a union of equals, each bringing their own completeness (and their own flaws and weirdness) to the table.

Let's bring this down to earth with a classic scenario: assembling an IKEA dresser (yes, it's the perfect microcosm of couple dynamics). Partner A meticulously lays out every screw and dowel, determined to follow the instructions step by step. Partner B, confident and impatient, eyeballs the pieces and declares, "I think I see how it goes together, instructions be damned." This is a make-or-break moment, folks. Will they complement each other's approach or combust? Best case, they joke through it – laughing when they realize the drawer is upside down, trading silly banter about who would survive longer on a desert island of Allen wrenches. Worst case, one storms off after accusing the other of being "impossible to work with!" The truth is, real couples bicker and negotiate and figure stuff out. It doesn't mean they're not soulmates; it means they're human. Successful couples aren't those who never fight or never expose their gaps; they're the ones who learn to fight fair and fill the gaps in practical ways ("I absolutely cannot decipher these illustrated instructions, honey, can you try while I make us some coffee?"). Heck, some counselors even suggest that the ability to cooperatively build

IKEA furniture is a decent indicator of relationship health. Couples who can laugh off the missing screw or the extra Allen key (why is there always an extra?) tend to have stronger relationships. It's not that they *complete* each other; it's that they support each other. One person's good at spatial assembly, the other's good at keeping morale high with jokes and pizza breaks – together they get the job done, with all shelves relatively level.

Beyond home-improvement fiascos, the "you complete me" myth can set up unrealistic expectations that your partner will fill every void – emotional, social, etc. – and that if you feel lonely or upset, it's their job to fix it. Real life gives that notion a reality check pretty fast. Maybe one of you has anxiety, or one of you is a slob while the other is neat. You'll quickly learn that no amount of true love instantly tidies the living room or cures lifelong insecurities. Instead of magically fixing each other's issues, couples often find they must navigate them patiently. One of the funniest (and healthiest) realizations is that you can love someone deeply and still find them incredibly annoying at times. The rom-coms rarely show the heroine rolling her eyes because her beloved is chewing too loudly, or the hero gently saying "I love you, but please, for the love of sanity, stop leaving wet towels on the bed." These little frictions don't mean you're incomplete or incompatible; they mean you're normal. Two "complete" people will inevitably have differences and annoyances. The key is being able to say, "I'm a whole person, you're a whole person – and sometimes our wholes get on each other's nerves, but we choose to stick together anyway."

A great illustration of real couple dynamics is attempting a DIY project or navigating a crisis together. It's messy and it definitely isn't like the movies. Take painting a room: You both end up with paint in your hair, the color looks different than the sample (cue mild blame-shifting: "Who picked this shade of green?!"), and you spend an afternoon in sweaty old clothes slapping paint on walls. By the end, you're exhausted and splotchy, but the room is painted – *and you did it together.* There's a proud, goofy grin you share in that moment. It's better than a perfect scene of movie dialogue, because it's real. Real love looks like teamwork, not dependence. It's splitting the IKEA hex key duties, it's tag-teaming the quest to fix the Wi-Fi at midnight when it goes down, it's one person calming the other's road rage during a traffic jam by telling a ridiculous joke. It's even having the courage to let your partner struggle with something on their own when they need to – because you're each other's partner, not each other's parent or therapist.

Perhaps the ultimate proof that "you complete me" is a myth is how couples handle the tough stuff. When life throws stress or grief your way, your partner can't wave a wand and make you whole or happy – but they can hold your hand through it. Instead of codependency (which is what Jerry's line basically glorifies), healthy love leans into interdependence. That means you support each other, rely on each other for comfort and care, but you don't lose your individual selves. You're like two separate trees with intertwined roots – standing strong together, but each with your own trunk. You don't become one tree (yikes, what a tangled mutant that would be); you grow side by side. In daily life, this might look like: you each have your own hobbies and friends, yet you also have your shared activities and mutual friends. You can spend a day apart doing your own thing and come back with stories to share. You don't expect your partner to love *everything* you love or fill *every* need you have – that's why we also have family, friends, and internal strength. As a wise reflection on that Jerry Maguire moment puts it, *we should aim to be two "I"s that form a "we," rather than two halves of one whole.* It's healthier and, ultimately, a lot more fun.

And for the record, assembling IKEA furniture or surviving any DIY project as a couple practically deserves its own merit badge in the relationship hall of fame. If you and your significant other can get through a full afternoon of Allen-wrench gymnastics without murdering each other, congratulations – you're demonstrating adaptability, patience, and teamwork. Who needs Prince Charming on a horse when you have a partner who will kneel on the floor next to you, squint at a page of cryptic pictograms, and say, "Okay love, let's figure this out together"? That right there is the real-life version of romantic heroism. It may come with extra screws and a few swear words, but it's infinitely more satisfying than any "you complete me" fantasy. Because at the end of the day, it's better to be complete on your own and then find someone to laugh with in the incompleteness of everyday life – to love not as two halves making a whole, but as two wholes making a whole lot of memories (and occasionally a whole lot of mess).

Happily Ever After (The Fine Print)

In the fairy tales, the story conveniently ends at the wedding – Cinderella and the Prince tie the knot, and then come those famous last words: *"and they lived happily ever after."* Roll credits, close the book. Ever wonder why we never get a sequel about what happens next? Well, as many a married couple can tell you with a sigh or a chuckle, it's because the real adventure begins after the honeymoon, and it's not always postcard material. There's a reason fairy tales end at the wedding scene: what comes after is a mix of mundane routine, occasional squabbles, and lots of unglamorous fine print that doesn't make for a neat storybook ending. If the Grimm Brothers had written *Marriage: The Later Years*, it might include riveting chapters like *"The Great Toothpaste Cap War,"* *"Laundry Mountain: This Time It's Personal,"* and *"The Kingdom of the Lost Socks."*

So, what does happily ever after really look like once the rice is swept off the pavement and the thank-you cards are mailed? For many, it looks like two people in sweatpants debating whether the toilet seat should be left up or down. It involves arguing over seemingly ridiculous things — the archetypal example being that infamous toothpaste cap. (Who knew so much marital strife could be packed into a tiny plastic tube top?) Maybe one of you can't stand when the cap is left off and the toothpaste crusts over, while the other swears they were totally going to put it back on later. From the outside, these spats seem comical — and frankly, they are. Yet, they happen. A lot. In one survey, nearly *80% of couples* reported having disagreements about chores and household duties, which includes plenty of quibbling over *how* things are done — like where the toothpaste is squeezed from (middle-squeezer vs. end-squeezer is practically a personality test), or why on earth it's so hard to replace the toilet paper roll when it's finished (*such* a classic). These little annoyances are the fine print of "in sickness and in health, in triumph and in triviality." The toothpaste cap fight isn't really about the cap, of course – therapists will say it's about feeling heard or respecting each other's preferences or some deeper need. But in the moment, it sure feels like it's about the cap, and heaven help the person who casually says "it's not a big deal" to the partner for whom it clearly is.

Real love's journey tends to wander through territory that fairy tales skip entirely: boredom, routine, and the occasional outright frustration. Think about it – fairy tales give us the chase, the courtship, maybe a hard-won union, and then they bow out. They don't show Snow White and her Prince a year later, dealing with the Prince leaving his boots in the hallway for the umpteenth time or Snow White's bizarre penchant for adopting every stray animal (the castle is literally full of pigeons now). They don't show Belle and the Beast (post-transformation) having a tense discussion about whose turn it is to blow out the candles and lock up the enchanted castle at night. But real couples know that after the big romantic milestones comes the long stretch of everyday living – and that's where the real work (and real fun, in a weird way) happens. One witty writer quipped that *marriage is work, and anyone who says otherwise is either not married or still in the honeymoon phase.* Ain't that the truth. The honeymoon phase, that blissful period when your partner's quirks seem charming and you can't imagine ever getting annoyed with each other, by definition doesn't last forever (typically it lasts months to a couple of years at most). Eventually, the spell lifts and you both realize that the person you love is, well, a person – a wonderful person, yes, but one with habits and moods that might drive you batty on occasion.

There's often a *moment of truth* in every long-term relationship where the rose-colored glasses come off. It might be the day you notice that your beloved chews cereal with a noise like a wood chipper, or the day you realize they think "cleaning the bathroom" means a quick wipe of the sink and nothing more. According to psychologists, as the dopamine rush of new love settles, our brains start to notice what we blissfully tuned out before. The flaws come into focus: the snoring that sounds like a freight train, the way they hum off-key in the shower, the differing opinions on the proper direction of toilet paper roll (over vs. under – a debate for the ages). And then there are the bigger life phases that can get, frankly, boring or stressful: endless days of working and paying bills, caring for children or aging parents, dealing with one or both partners' career pressures, health scares, mortgages, the whole nine yards. This is the stuff you don't see in rom-coms because it's not neatly resolved in a two-hour plot – it's ongoing. Love doesn't hit a peak and freeze-frame; it evolves through the doldrums and chaos of life.

Does that sound a bit daunting or dreary? Perhaps. But here's the flip side: happily ever after is not a static destination; it's a journey, bumps and all. Those fairy tale writers left out the fine print that even the best couples will have bad days. They will argue – maybe not about evil witches or forbidden love, but about whether it's worth paying extra for organic milk, or how someone *never* remembers to close the garage door. They will have phases where romance takes a backseat because life is demanding – like when you're up every two hours with a newborn and romance becomes giving each other a bleary-eyed high-five for surviving another night. They will encounter times when one or both partners feel

19

disillusioned, wondering "is this it?" when faced with a spouse who's in a months-long funk or when the highlight of the week is the new episode of a TV show you watch together in silence. These moments don't mean the love story is broken; they mean it's real and still in progress. It's during these unexciting or challenging times that couples often discover a deeper, quieter kind of love – one built not on constant excitement but on trust, commitment, and yes, humor.

Humor is a lifesaver in the ever after. The couples who make it through decades tend to be the ones who can laugh at the absurdity of their recurring squabbles. They develop a kind of short-hand comedy routine about their issues: "Oh, here we go, the Great Thermostat Battle of 2025, round 3!" or "Attention, please: The mystery of the Missing Remote has once again rocked our household." It's not that they're making fun of each other (okay, maybe gently they are), but they're making fun of the situation – diffusing tension with a shared smile. I know a couple who playfully keep score of who's the bigger neat freak, with a whiteboard on the fridge tallying "crumb crimes" (apparently one of them is forever leaving crumbs on the counter, and the other finds it endlessly and amusingly criminal). Another pair I'm acquainted with has a running joke that their marriage is sponsored by Google Calendar – because without syncing their schedules and reminders, their life would fall apart. Instead of resenting the mundanity, they've leaned into it with humor.

Of course, some days will test your patience without any laughter in sight. You might feel more like growling "I'm just *not* feeling the happily in this ever after right now." But the beauty of long-term love is in its resilience. The fairy tale ideal would have us believe that a perfect couple never fights and never falters after the wedding. Reality says, *nonsense.* Strong couples might fight over and over about the same stupid thing (insert *toothpaste cap/ trash not taken out/ directions refusal* here), but over time, they learn to fight better, or at least to apologize quicker. They learn each other's triggers – maybe the wife realizes that the husband's grumpiness about the toothpaste is really about feeling unappreciated for the other cleaning he did, and the husband realizes the wife's nagging about his phone use is because she misses talking to him. In other words, they slowly get better at reading the footnotes of their conflicts. Relationship experts note that repetitive small fights usually mask deeper themes of power, care, or respect. Couples who figure that out can start addressing the real issues ("I need you to show me you care by helping out more," or "I feel disrespected when you do X"), instead of just yelling about the toilet seat. It's like unlocking a new level in the video game of marriage – suddenly the final boss isn't the cap-less toothpaste, it's the underlying feeling of being taken for granted, and that's something you can tackle as a team once you see it.

Let's also consider that "ever after" implies a long, long time – potentially decades. Over such a span, *everything* won't be happy. But a lot of it can be pretty great, even in an ordinary way. Many older couples will tell you that contentment in a long relationship comes from a collection of small daily pleasures rather than constant fireworks. It's in the comfortable silence of two people reading books in the same room. It's in the routine of a goodbye kiss every morning, even when you're rushed.

It's in knowing exactly how your partner likes their tea and making it for them without asking. Those things never make it into the fairy tale version, but they are its real foundation. There's a certain magic in knowing someone so well that you can predict their bad jokes, or in having a vault of shared memories and silly anecdotes that no one else would find funny but crack both of you up.

One of the best-kept secrets of "happily ever after" is that the mundane can be deeply meaningful. That fight over the toothpaste? It might, oddly enough, bring you closer after you resolve it for the fiftieth time, because each time you understand each other a bit more. The boring Tuesday nights doing nothing special? Those are threads in the tapestry of your life together – you may look back fondly on the simple comfort of those nights. A long journey with someone will inevitably have highs (celebrations, romantic getaways, triumphs) and lows (losses, illnesses, disappointments) – but a lot of middle, too. Embracing the middle ground is key. When fairy tales end at the wedding, they miss the opportunity to show that the *real* happily ever after is an ongoing choice. Every day, couples wake up and, as one writer said, "actively choose that person" again, even when they're annoying, even when life is dull or hard. That daily re-commitment is both work and a wonder.

So, if you're living your own love story and sometimes worry that it's not measuring up to the storybooks, fear not. The fine print of happily ever after might read something like: *"They argued occasionally, sometimes about very silly things. They faced a few dragons that weren't in the original script (deadlines, illnesses, financial stress). They went through phases when things were routine and uneventful. But they always had each other's back, they learned and grew, and they found joy in the little moments. And yes, they loved each other deeply — not every single second (because that's impossible), but in sum total, day after day, year after year."* That's a pretty good ever after, if you ask me. It might not be storybook perfect, but it's real and it's rich with authenticity.

In the end, maybe we should rewrite that fairy-tale phrase from "happily ever after" to "messily ever after, with love." The happiness isn't a permanent state you magically achieve — it's sprinkled throughout the journey, in between the messes and mundane tasks. The princess and prince of reality don't ride off into a sunset freeze-frame; they ride into a lifetime of sunrises and sunsets together — some breathtaking, some cloudy, but together. And if they're lucky (and have a good sense of humor), they'll find that reality, with all its dirty dishes and credit scores and toothpaste squabbles, can be far more satisfying than the fantasy. Because when love meets reality, it isn't the end of the story — it's the beginning of a far more interesting, funny, and rewarding one. And they lived, imperfectly yet contentedly, ever after.

Chapter 2

The Toilet Seat War and Other Domestic Battlegrounds

Introduction: Every long-term couple knows that love alone doesn't conquer all – certainly not the skirmishes over mundane household habits. Research shows that the average couple has around 312 arguments a year over petty issues, from soggy towels to channel surfing. In fact, minor domestic annoyances account for the *majority* of conflicts in many relationships. These "battles" may seem trivial to outsiders, but to those in the trenches, a raised toilet seat or an unemptied dishwasher can feel like a declaration of war. Below, we delve into four notorious domestic battlegrounds – with stats, studies, and real examples that prove you're not alone in these fights (and perhaps provide some comic relief along the way).

The Toilet Seat Standoff

Few household spats are as iconic as the toilet seat showdown. It's a classic he-said/she-said (or rather, *seat-up vs. seat-down*) dispute that has inspired countless sitcom jokes and even academic papers. Surveys confirm this gripe is nearly universal: leaving the toilet seat up ranks as the second most common household annoyance for cohabiting couples, outranked only by leaving lights on. One poll of 2,000 adults found that such *"bathroom wars"* are widespread – seven in ten couples admitted to arguing about the state of the bathroom, with the up/down position of the toilet seat cited as a frequent flashpoint. It's not just playful bickering either; nearly one in five people have ended a relationship over a partner's atrocious bathroom behavior (yes, *really*). The humble porcelain throne, it seems, can be a minefield for modern love.

On the surface, the toilet seat debate appears to boil down to simple physics: one partner's convenience versus the other's comfort. But psychologists and marriage counselors argue it symbolizes something deeper. Leaving the seat up after your partner has begged you to leave it down is often taken as a sign of disrespect or selfishness – essentially a miniature referendum on whether you're thinking in terms of "we" or "me". As therapist Dr. Becky Whetstone notes, the issue usually isn't *really* about the toilet at all, but about feeling considered (or ignored) by one's partner. No wonder an exasperated spouse might say, "It's not the seat, it's what it *represents*!" – namely, the *basic courtesy* of not leaving your loved one to take an unexpected 3 A.M. plunge.

Cultural gender norms fuel this standoff. Polls show women care far more about the seat position than men do: nearly 23% of women cited "toilet seat left up" as a top household complaint, compared to only 8% of men. Perhaps that's because women are often the "victims" of the surprise midnight dunk, whereas many men simply shrug at the issue. This disparity can turn the toilet into contested territory in a shared home. It has even led to some tongue-in-cheek *scholarly* analyses: believe it or not, economists and game theorists have published papers on the optimal toilet seat strategy. One 17-page study by a Michigan State economist mathematically concluded that if women in the house equal or outnumber men, the rational solution is to always leave the seat down (much to no one's surprise). Another paper modeled the toilet seat dilemma as a game, finding that while the "always down" rule is technically inefficient (it maximizes total seat motions), it may be the equilibrium that minimizes yelling – a classic case of minimizing household *discord* over maximizing efficiency. In short, even PhDs side with the "down" camp, if only to keep domestic peace.

Despite the lighthearted studies and comedic memes, the toilet seat war rages on in households worldwide. It's entrenched enough to be a pop-culture cliché – the kind of squabble parodied in sitcoms and debated in Twitter threads. One humor writer likened the debate to the "is a hot dog a sandwich?" genre of viral arguments: objectively petty, yet oddly capable of igniting outsized passion. Indeed, what starts as a quibble over a seat can escalate into a full-blown fight about *consideration, fairness, and respect.* As one frustrated wife told her husband, "If I can put it up for you, you can put it down for me!" – to which the husband inevitably retorts, "Why is *your* way the default?" Round and round it goes. The wise couples eventually learn that a two-second seat adjustment (or investing in a slow-close lid) is far easier than waging endless battle. For everyone else, this minor cold war continues – proof that sometimes, the smallest things at home cause the biggest standoffs.

Blanket Hoggers, Snorers, and Thermostat Tyrants

Sleeping in the same bed was supposed to be romantic – until you spend the night fighting for a scrap of blanket, shielding your ears from thunderous snores, or sweating because your partner insists the room be 80°F. Welcome to the nocturnal battlefront of cohabitation, where the enemy is not your beloved, but their baffling bedtime habits. Research reveals that *nighttime annoyances* are incredibly common and can seriously strain a relationship. In one wide-ranging UK survey, a whopping 83% of couples reported at least one partner snores, and 82% said one person is prone to thrashing around or "tossing and turning" in bed. It's no wonder that the concept of a "sleep divorce" – sleeping in separate beds or rooms – has gained traction. A 2024 American Academy of Sleep Medicine poll found that 29% of Americans have opted to regularly sleep apart from their partner just to get a decent night's rest. Far from signaling marital doom, experts say this can be a practical truce: "It's not about ending a relationship – it's about prioritizing sleep health" and avoiding resentment over constant fatigue.

Graph: "Mattress wars" – A YouGov poll found 57% of couples feel they share the bed fairly, but 27% say they get less than their fair share (i.e. one partner hogs space/blankets). Bad bedtime behaviors are rampant: snoring is the most common complaint (reported in 83% of couples), and blanket-hogging is so prevalent that 36% of women admit to stealing covers, versus 23% of men.

Aside from space, blanket hogging is a leading cause of nocturnal discord. Anyone who's woken up shivering at 2 A.M. while their partner is cocooned in all the blankets can relate. In fact, about 35% of people say they sleep with a "cover hog" partner. One quirky study even calculated that blanket thieves get the better end of the deal: "cover hogs" log an extra 6 minutes of sleep per night on average compared to their chilly counterparts. (Small comfort when you're the one left blanket-less!) To cope, some couples try the *"Scandinavian sleep method"* – separate duvets on the same bed – which 1 in 10 people have embraced as a way to end the tug-of-war peacefully. And for truly desperate cases, separate beds may beckon; recent surveys show over a third of couples at least occasionally sleep in different rooms, by choice or necessity. It's a testament to how seriously people value sleep: they'll rearrange the entire night routine to avoid the midnight battle of the blanket.

Snoring, of course, is the other bedtime bugbear that has driven many to the couch (or to consider smothering their partner with a pillow, half-jokingly). Statistically, men are far more likely to be the culprit: about 63% of men in one survey confessed to snoring, versus 46% of women. (Women snore too, but at least they're less proud of it.) The same poll found 70% of couples endure the lovely habit of one partner passing gas in their sleep – a detail that might make you laugh unless you're the one trapped under the covers with a "thermostat tyrant" who also *dutch-ovens* you. Indeed, men were about 12 percentage points more likely to admit to *breaking wind between the sheets* than women, proving that Mother Nature has a sense of humor in whom she bestows these charms. All these sleep disturbances take a toll: in a survey of 800 people, 44% of those who share a bed said their partner's sleep habits have made them question the relationship – nearly half! It's both funny and a little tragic that loud snores and midnight elbow jabs can shake the foundations of an otherwise loving union.

Then there's the infamous thermostat battle, which often extends beyond the bedroom to the entire home climate. If one of you is always freezing under three blankets while the other flips the AC to arctic mode, you're not alone. A Vivint Solar survey found 75% of American couples argue over the thermostat setting. In these "thermostat wars," stealth tactics are common: 64% admitted to secretly adjusting the temperature behind their partner's back to suit their own comfort. And heaven forbid someone actually *touches* the thermostat unannounced – 60% of people said they get angry when their partner changes the thermostat without asking. It's practically a domestic cardinal sin. Perhaps this is why one partner (stereotypically the one who's always cold) earns the label "thermostat tyrant," guarding the control like the Iron Throne. Meanwhile, the perpetually warm partner plots in the shadows, waiting for a chance to nudge it down a degree. The struggle is so common that some HVAC companies and advice columns now offer tips on brokering a "climate compromise" in the home. Until that détente is reached, couples will continue engaging in this absurd power struggle over a single degree on the dial (sometimes literally – many a quarrel has been waged over setting it to 71°F vs. 72°F).

From snoring to stealing covers to thermostat sabotage, these nighttime and household comfort issues prove that intimacy isn't always romantic – sometimes it's ridiculous. The good news? Solutions exist (white-noise machines, earplugs, dual blankets, smart thermostats, etc.), and plenty of couples laugh it off and adapt. The bad news: if you're dealing with a champion snorer or a blanket bandit, your sleep might be in for some *interesting* interruptions. Consider it one more test of love's endurance: *Can our relationship survive without central heating set to tropical?* For three-quarters of couples fighting over the thermostat, the answer, with compromise (or separate comforters), is hopefully yes.

Chore Wars: The Empire Strikes Back

Sharing a life also means sharing a living space – and all the unglamorous work that comes with it. This is where the "chore wars" commence. Dividing household chores has long been a sore spot for couples, and despite progress in gender roles, research shows it's still a *highly combustible* issue. In fact, polls consistently rank housework as one of the top things couples fight about, right up there with money and sex. A 2019 Pew Research survey found that 56% of married Americans believe sharing household chores is "very important" for a successful marriage, reflecting just how weighty the issue is in our collective psyche. When chores feel imbalanced, resentment brews quickly. It doesn't take a marriage counselor to predict what happens when one partner feels like the live-in maid while the other "forgets" that dishes don't wash themselves.

Chart: Who actually does the housework? A Gallup survey illustrates the traditional division of chores in heterosexual U.S. couples. Women reported doing the majority of tasks like laundry, cleaning, and cooking (dark green bars), while men more often handled things like car maintenance and yardwork (light green bars). Gray segments show the minority of couples who split tasks equally.

Despite changes in society, the gender gap in housework remains alive and well. According to Gallup and Pew data, women still shoulder a larger share of domestic duties in most couples – and they *know* it. A majority of women (59%) say they do more household chores than their partner, while only a measly 6% say their partner does more. Men, on the other hand, often don't see the imbalance: nearly half of men (46%) insist that the chores are split about equally. This perception gulf can be comical if it weren't a bit infuriating. (It calls to mind the classic scenario: Husband, genuinely bewildered, says "Honey, I do plenty around the house!" while Wife stares in disbelief, mentally cataloguing the countless tasks he seems oblivious to.) Earlier research echoes this: back in 2010, a "Chore Wars" report found 69% of women felt they did most of the housework, whereas 53% of men claimed *they* did as much as or more than their spouse. In other words, many men think they're pulling their weight while many women would beg to differ – a discrepancy that itself can spark arguments.

And argue they do. Surveys indicate that chores are a frequent trigger for conflict. One poll found 1 in 5 couples actively argue about household chores at least once a month, and a significant number skirmish far more often. A UK study commissioned by a cleaning products firm found that 39% of people said most of their spats with their partner stem from disagreements over cleaning and chores, and 13% admitted to fighting about chores on a daily basis. (Daily! That's exhaustion by a thousand cuts – or perhaps by a thousand *unwashed dishes*.) Even more sobering, three in five respondents – 59% – in that survey said that constant domestic disagreements had pushed their relationship to the brink of collapse at times. Clearly, chore distribution isn't just a minor annoyance; for many, it strikes at the heart of fairness and partnership in a relationship. Little wonder that "Did you remember to take out the trash?" can escalate into a fiery exchange of "I do everything around here!" and "Oh really? What about the time I cleaned the entire garage – five years ago?!"

One particularly contentious aspect of chore wars is the persistence of traditional roles. Data show women still tend to handle the day-to-day indoor chores: in 2019, 58% of women said they are primarily responsible for laundry, 51% for cleaning the house, and 51% for meal prep, far outpacing the men who take those on. Men, by contrast, more often take charge of tasks like yardwork (59% of men mainly do this) and car maintenance (69% of men) – jobs that, while important, usually aren't daily needs. This can lead to a mismatch in perceptions: the husband feels he *does* contribute (mowing the lawn on Saturday and tinkering with the car), yet the wife is drowning daily in less visible but relentless chores like laundry, dishes, cooking, and childcare. Over time, such imbalance (or the feeling of it) breeds frustration. The pandemic era didn't fully fix it either. By 2020, men were actually *more* satisfied with their chore split than pre-pandemic – 55% of husbands said they were very satisfied with how chores were divided, up from 49% before – whereas only 38% of wives felt very satisfied. Translation: a lot of guys thought, *"This is fine,"* while their wives silently thought, *"This is nowhere near fine."* The "Empire" of entrenched gender norms *strikes back*, indeed.

Now, not all chore disputes end in stalemate. Some couples negotiate solutions – hiring a cleaner, delegating specific tasks, or instituting the classic "whoever cooks, the other cleans" rule. Many modern pairs strive for a more equal partnership than their parents had, and there is gradual change. Gallup notes that since 1996, men are doing a bit more than before (women's share of tasks like grocery shopping, laundry, and dishwashing has declined ~10 percentage points as those duties are increasingly shared or taken up by men). But progress is slow, and expectations often collide. There are also cultural stereotypes adding fuel: think of the trope of the nagging wife or the bumbling husband who claims incompetence at ironing so he never has to do it. These can become self-fulfilling prophecies (the husband does a half-hearted job, the wife "re-does" it, and resentment grows). Chore wars can escalate from small gripes to symbolizing larger issues of respect, equality, and effort. For example, a pile of his dirty socks on the floor isn't just a mess – to her, it might scream "I assume you'll pick these up, because *I* certainly won't," which feels an awful lot like taking your partner for granted.

Humorously, couples often keep score in these battles like warring factions. ("I vacuumed last week and the week before, so why can't you do it *this* week?" "Sure, you vacuum, but I'm the only one who cleans the bathroom!") The negotiation never ends. One survey even found that some 20% of couples believe the secret to harmony is separate bathrooms altogether – essentially, a chore demilitarized zone – and 17% said if they could afford it, they'd opt for separate bedrooms too! That's right, a subset of people think the key to a happy relationship is *strategic avoidance* of each other's mess. It might actually work for some, but for most of us, we have to learn to collaborate in the same space. In the end, winning the chore war likely requires the opposite of "striking back" –

instead, calling a truce. As one piece of expert advice in *Psychology Today* quips, pick your battles: don't die on the hill of every little pet peeve, and discuss only one or two major complaints at a time – nicely. Keeping score like it's a zero-sum game will drive you both mad. After all, in a true partnership, *when one person loses (or is exhausted and embittered), neither really wins*. So whether it's instituting a chore chart, embracing imperfection, or just sincerely thanking your partner for emptying the dishwasher, any small step to ease tensions is worth it. Otherwise, as the stats show, chore wars can become a Death Star that blows up a happy home from within.

Can't Live With 'Em, Can't Get 'Em to Do the Laundry

This tongue-in-cheek section title says it all: loving someone means accepting that, at times, they will drive you utterly crazy. The reality of cohabitation is that everyone has quirks and annoying habits, and those little things – the "domestic battlegrounds" that aren't full-blown fights, but constant irritants – require patience (and often, a sense of humor) to survive. Think *floordrobe*: that charming habit where clothes never make it into closets or drawers, instead forming a semi-permanent carpet on the bedroom floor. Or the particular way your partner loads the dishwasher like a chaotic evil Tetris game, or their tendency to leave empty containers in the fridge, as if an empty milk jug chilling next to actual food serves any purpose. These micro-annoyances rarely show up in rom-coms, but they are the bread and butter of real relationships. As one Reddit user lamented about their spouse, "I love them to bits, but if I find one more dirty sock under the couch, I might scream." It's the *little stuff* that truly tests the mantra *"can't live with 'em, can't live without 'em."*

Studies and surveys have attempted to catalog these everyday grievances. A British survey of 3,000 people (aptly reported by a bathroom retail company) found that the "majority" of couples' 312 annual arguments stem from minor irritations – things like *not replacing the empty toilet paper roll, leaving the toilet seat up, scattering wet towels or dirty laundry on the floor, cluttering surfaces with used tissues,* or letting hair clog up the shower drain. In a list of the top 30 cohabiting-couple quarrels, alongside the big ones (chores, money) are gems such as leaving dirty clothes on the floor, dropping crumbs in the bed, not dusting properly, and not making the bed in the morning. Even "crumbs on the sofa" and "dishes left to 'soak' for ages" make the list. These little habits can drive your partner up the wall. Why? Possibly because they happen *every single day.* One lone sock on the floor isn't a relationship killer, but the 500th sock left strewn about begins to feel like an act of war (or at least, an act of willful obliviousness). Over time, couples either address these peeves or develop a tolerance for them – ideally laughing about them rather than fighting. As one marriage expert put it, *not* every molehill needs to become a mountain; sometimes you've got to "let some stuff slide" for the greater good of the relationship.

Real-world examples of petty domestic strife abound, often shared humorously on social media or advice columns. There's the viral tale of the spouse who kept relocating the TV remote to bizarre places (like the fridge) out of habit, leaving the other utterly perplexed. Or the wife who posted a photo of her refrigerator containing an empty plate covered in foil – courtesy of her husband – captioned: "Behold, the leftover that wasn't." (He had eaten the cake but put the empty plate back in the fridge, as if the ghost of dessert might still be there. Why? We may never know.) For every bizarre quirk, there's an equal and opposite complaint: one partner's *"fridge quirks"* might be another's ingenious system. Perhaps he alphabetizes condiments and loses it when she puts ketchup next to mustard *out of order*. Perhaps she labels every food item with the date, and he finds it overkill. These things can bewilder you because they're so far from *your* "normal." Cohabitation is essentially the collision of two "normals," and the debris field includes all these little tiffs over how things *ought* to be done.

Another modern twist: technology and pop culture have introduced new arenas for annoyance. "Netflix cheating" – the act of watching a shared favorite show alone, ahead of your partner – has certainly led to a few icy stares. Smartphone habits are another: a Pew survey noted that 25% of partnered adults felt their significant other was regularly distracted by their phone when they were together. And let's not forget the classic thermostat fight we covered, or its cousin: the speaker volume war (where one loves blasting music while the other craves quiet). Every era of cohabitation has its unique friction points. In the 2020s, that might mean arguing about whose turn it is to fill the Wi-Fi router with the latest firmware update or grousing that your partner's Alexa routines are driving you nuts at 6 AM.

So, how do couples cope with the endless parade of small annoyances without losing their minds (or their love for each other)? The key seems to be learning which battles to fight and which to laugh off. Relationship counselors often advise communicating kindly about the habits that truly bother you, and letting the truly trivial stuff go unpunished. For instance, if your boyfriend perpetually runs a "floordrobe," you might designate a *no-judgment zone* (a chair or corner) for his semi-clean clothes, rather than nag him daily to use a hanger. If your wife leaves the kitchen cabinets open like a poltergeist, maybe gently joke about starting a "close the cabinet" fund (drop a quarter each time, go out to dinner when it's full). Many couples develop a playful shorthand for their irritations – a light ribbing that says "I noticed, but I still love you." One husband shared that when his wife inevitably leaves the dish sponge sopping wet on the counter, he'll hold it up and say with a grin, "Present from the Sponge Fairy again?" It defuses the tension, and she good-naturedly tries to remember next time. In long-term relationships, a bit of humor and grace go a long way. After all, you likely have your own weird habits that your partner tolerates in return.

At the end of the day, those domestic battlegrounds – the toilet seat stand-offs, blanket tug-of-wars, chore melees, and laundry list of pet peeves – are part and parcel of sharing your life (and home) with someone. They're the unsexy, unromantic underside of intimacy. Yet, navigating them successfully can *strengthen* a couple's bond. Each time you avoid a blow-up over an unmade bed or calmly address the fact that you're the only one who buys toilet paper, you're basically saying, *"I value us more than this little annoyance."* As one wise (and likely long-married) person put it: *Marriage is finding that one special someone you can annoy for the rest of your life – and who will still stick around.* Embracing that truth with a smile (and maybe a chore chart) might just be the secret to lasting domestic peace. In the grand saga of love, these trivial battles are comic relief – maddening in the moment, but memories you'll chuckle about later. And if all else fails, you can always invest in two bathrooms and a really big blanket. Just saying.

Chapter 3
Pillow Talk and Dirty Little Secrets

The White Lie Lowdown

Every long-term couple has a secret hall of fame of little fibs. Maybe it's the enthusiastic nod you give when your spouse asks if you *love* their kale-cucumber smoothie (the one that tastes like liquefied lawn clippings). Or perhaps it's the "Wow, honey, your Excel spreadsheet looks fascinating!" you exclaim while secretly fighting off a yawn. If this sounds familiar, congratulations – you're fluent in the universal language of white lies. And you're far from alone. In fact, research finds that romantic partners lie to each other about three times per week on average. These aren't evil betrayals but usually *"harmless"* untruths deployed to keep the peace and spare feelings.

Psychologists sometimes call this "deceptive affection," where you express fondness you don't fully feel, like complimenting a bad haircut or saying "I'm not mad" when you're seething. We do it because constant brutal honesty is *overrated* – even the experts admit *"we don't always want to know the truth all the time"*. A little faked cheerfulness can save us from needless squabbles and hurt feelings.

Sure, honesty matters in the big picture, but let's be real: telling your spouse their new quarantine mustache looks *"distinguished"* (when it actually resembles a small furry caterpillar) is often kinder than honesty.

These minor falsifications are the relationship equivalent of Instagram filters – smoothing out imperfections for the sake of everyone's overall enjoyment.

Modern love is practically built on such polite pretenses. Think of the everyday lies couples tell:

- Complimenting questionable choices: *"That tie-dye shirt is so stylish!"* (Instead of admitting it hurts your retinas.)

- Feigning interest: *"Tell me more about that Level 60 achievement in your video game, babe – I'm all ears!"* (Said no one ever, but we try.)

These little deceptions act as social glue. Studies have found that the most common motivation for white lies in romance is to avoid conflict or spare your partner's feelings. In other words, we lie *because* we love. As communication professor Sean Horan, who studied affectionate fibbing, explains, people often fake a smile or a compliment to maintain the relationship's happiness. Horan put it best: *"We don't always want to know the truth all the time."* And honestly – pun intended – can you blame us?

Life is hard enough without hearing every unfiltered thought that pops into your beloved's head. Imagine a world where couples were 100% frank:

- *"Yes, your poem is a bit terrible."*

- *"I really don't care how your work meeting went, it's boring."*

- *"By the way, I did throw out that ugly old T-shirt of yours."*

That world would be a fast track to Splitsville. Instead, a sprinkle of sugar-coated deceit keeps things running smoothly. Of course, balance is key – telling your partner *"I paid the electric bill"* when you didn't is not the same as saying *"Dinner was great"* when it was mediocre. Lying about serious issues (money troubles, secret vices, actual infidelity) is toxic. But fibbing that their over-salted pasta was "restaurant quality"? That's just good manners.

In the end, strategic deception sometimes beats brutal honesty in a relationship. A dash of white lie here and there is like putting padding on the sharp corners of truth. It prevents unnecessary pain. As one witty blogger quipped, *truth is like sunlight – we need it to grow, but if we stand in it naked all day we'll get burned.* So go ahead, tell your significant other that their burnout artisanal donut venture is a brilliant idea (even if you have doubts). They'll feel supported, you'll avoid a fight, and no one gets hurt. That's the *lowdown* on white lies: when used wisely, everybody wins (and nobody has to gag on a kale smoothie).

Secret Single Behaviors (SSB)

Moving in together is the grand reveal, the moment the curtain lifts on all the bizarre little habits you *thought* you hid so well. There's even a term for those solo quirks we conceal from partners: Secret Single Behavior (SSB). Originally coined on *Sex and the City*, SSB refers to the weird, wonderful rituals people indulge in only when alone. Think of it as the *"me time"* performance art that no one else is meant to witness. That is, until cohabitation turns your private one-person show into a two-person audience.

Before sharing a roof, we all put our best foot forward. You might have meticulously concealed the fact that you sometimes eat dinner standing over the kitchen sink (why dirty a plate for salad when the sink is *right there?*). Perhaps you always made sure to hide evidence of your late-night Doritos-and-peanut-butter snacks. But once you and your partner get coupled up under one lease, the truth comes out. You walk in to find your darling singing improvised show tunes to the cat in a weird falsetto. They discover that you have a habit of leaving laundry *where it lands* (aka the "floordrobe"). Welcome to SSB paradise!

Let's be honest, we all have at least one ridiculous habit:

- Eating cereal out of a mixing bowl while binge-watching reality TV in pajamas.

- Keeping a floordrobe of clothes piled on *"the chair."*

- Using a ridiculous baby voice when talking to the dog.

- Wearing a face mask that makes you look like a swamp monster (only when no one's around, of course).

There are countless real-life examples. One woman confessed that her boyfriend will munch on dry tortellini straight out of the bag as a bedtime snack (yes, uncooked pasta crunching noisily at 11 PM). Perhaps your partner is one of those who undresses completely just to use the bathroom – a shock the first time you witness it, trust me.

When these secret single behaviors emerge, the results can be hilarious and enlightening. "No relationship remains unchanged after moving in together," as one witty writer noted – it's when you learn your partner's truest self, *the good, the bad, and yes, the ugly*. Initially, you might be equal parts amused and horrified. (*"Is he really eating ice cream out of a mug with a fork?" "Does she truly need four different shampoos in the shower?"*) These revelations can even be deal-breakers for some couples if the habits clash with core values of hygiene or sanity. But more often, they become the fodder for inside jokes and deeper intimacy.

Psychologically, exposing your weird habits is a sign that you feel comfortable with your partner – you trust them enough to let them see the *"real"* you (warts, onesies, midnight Cheeto binges and all). Cohabitation researchers note that this phase can be bumpy, but ultimately it's a milestone that can bring you closer. You learn to compromise: maybe you agree not to judge each other's odd routines, and in return, they promise not to live-tweet your 2 A.M. kitchen dance parties. Intimacy isn't just built on candlelight dinners; sometimes it's solidified by the shared knowledge that your boyfriend talks in his sleep and occasionally yells nonsense like "There's ice cream all over the stairs, bro!" in the dead of night.

The key to surviving SSB discoveries is humor and tolerance. Laugh about the quirks – humor turns shock into bonding. And practice some give-and-take: maybe insist they stop leaving wet towels on the bed, but acknowledge you have your own odd habits too. Over time, many couples develop a fondness for each other's oddities. That weird habit becomes a cute anecdote: *"Oh, that's just him, he has to watch YouTube videos to fall asleep."* You might even start adopting a few of their quirks yourself (couples who burp together, stay together?).

In summary, Secret Single Behaviors are the "dirty little secrets" that inevitably come out in cohabitation. It can be a shock to discover that the love of your life sometimes eats spaghetti with scissors or keeps a collection of Star Wars action figures in the bed. But if you handle it with patience and a sense of humor, those quirks can deepen your love (or at least give you great stories to tell). As the saying goes, *before you marry someone, you should first make them use a computer with slow internet to see who they really are.* Living together is kind of like that slow internet test – revealing, occasionally frustrating, but ultimately an adventure in true intimacy.

Snooping, Spying, and the Trust Bust

Now we turn to a less adorable dirty secret in relationships: the irresistible urge to snoop. You know the drill. Your partner's phone buzzes at 11 PM with a message from some *"Alex"*. They fall asleep, and there it is on the nightstand – their unlocked phone practically beckoning you. Your heart says, *"Respect their privacy,"* but your brain (and let's be honest, your nosy side) whispers, *"Just a quick peek, for peace of mind…"* In the digital age, snooping has never been easier – or more tempting.

If you've ever secretly checked a significant other's texts or browser history, you are definitely not alone. A Pew Research study found that about 34% of people in serious relationships have secretly checked their partner's phone. Yet roughly 70% of Americans insist that snooping through a partner's phone is unacceptable – a classic case of *"do as I say, not as I do."*

Technology has turned trust into a 24/7 surveillance opportunity. Beyond phones, there are now shared location apps that let lovers track each other's every move on a map. Some couples find this comforting or convenient (*"Can you grab milk since I see you're near Walmart?"*). Others find it creepy — a high-tech leash. Increasingly, couples even use location-sharing apps like Life360 to keep tabs on each other's whereabouts (checking in several times a day). Many say this makes the relationship feel more official, and a sizable number think refusing to share location is basically a red flag.

Of course, there's a dark side: if you always know your partner's location, you also know when they took an extra 20 minutes at "work" (was it actually a detour to the pub?). For the insecure, these apps can fuel anxious thoughts. And refusing to share location can itself raise suspicion. So much for trust being about *faith* — now it's more like *"trust, but verify."*

The tragicomic aspect of snooping is that it often *backfires*. If you dig, you may well find *something*: maybe actual evidence of wrongdoing, or maybe just something utterly mundane that *seems* suspicious out of context. One woman lamented that she snooped and discovered her boyfriend griping to a friend, unflatteringly comparing her to someone else. Ouch.

Even when snooping turns up nothing bad, you've now inhaled a lungful of guilt for violating your partner's privacy. You can't exactly say, *"Honey, I feel so much better after reading all your emails — you're totally not cheating!"* without admitting you breached their trust. So you stew in silence, which creates its own distance.

All of this begs the question: what does trust even mean now? It used to imply giving your partner the benefit of the doubt. Now it often means *proving* you have nothing to hide by granting full access to your life. In other words, trust has started to mean constant verification instead of faith. Indeed, one therapist warned that peeking at your partner's phone only feeds secrecy and distrust – a vicious cycle. You get insecure so you snoop, then you find something (or imagine you did), and trust erodes even further.

Now, a little mutual transparency isn't necessarily bad – sharing passwords or turning on location tracking *by mutual agreement* can be practical (like if one of you gets locked out or lost). The difference is consent and intent. Sharing info for convenience and safety is one thing; snooping or demanding access out of suspicion is quite another (that's a symptom of deeper trust issues).

Given how normal oversharing has become (think of couples who broadcast every detail on social media), the very idea of privacy in a partnership can feel blurred. Still, real trust requires boundaries. Trusting someone means you don't feel compelled to inspect their every DM, and they don't feel entitled to scour yours. As any reformed phone-snooper will tell you, the adrenaline rush of "finding the truth" is rarely worth the fallout.

If you feel the itch to snoop, remember the old proverb: *"Seek and ye shall find."* But once you pry something out, you can't un-find it. In the grand tapestry of love, snooping is a thread that, when pulled, can unravel the whole relationship. Handle with care – or better yet, address your worries with your partner openly *before* you go full James Bond on their phone.

True Confessions (and Why They're Overrated)

In our tell-all culture, there's a popular idea that total transparency is the key to a great relationship. We're encouraged to "never keep secrets" and to share every thought and feeling with our partners like they're our personal diary. Honesty *is* important – no one's arguing for deceit – but let's pump the brakes on the confessional zeal. Sometimes, full disclosure is less a noble act and more like using a shotgun to kill a mosquito: overkill with a lot of unintended damage.

Modern relationships often come with pressure to overshare. There's this belief that *"if you really love me, you'll tell me everything."* But do you really want to know *everything?* Does your husband truly need the play-by-play of every crush or flirtation you've ever had? Some thoughts are fleeting, some feelings are trivial or best left private. Blurting them out in the name of "openness" can cause unnecessary hurt. As *Psychology Today* put it, *radical honesty* – sharing every innermost thought – can lead to hurt feelings and selfish oversharing that benefits the speaker at the expense of the listener. In other words, just because something is true doesn't mean it's *helpful* to say.

Let's draw a line between healthy honesty and compulsive over-confession. Healthy honesty means telling your partner the important things that truly affect the relationship – say, *"I've been feeling unappreciated lately,"* or *"I messed up and kissed someone at a work party, and we should talk about it."* (Okay, that last one is a doozy, but arguably they deserve to know.) Compulsive over-sharing is blurting out things that only serve to ease your own guilt or anxiety, with no benefit to your partner. For example: *"I sometimes think your best friend is really attractive,"* or *"I had a dream about my ex last night."* Ask yourself – whose burden are you unloading with these confessions? Often, it's yours. You feel guilty or conflicted, so you spill your guts to your partner expecting forgiveness or understanding. But what you're really doing is handing *them* the burden of your guilt, or your random passing feelings, and now they have to live with that knowledge.

Emotional intelligence in relationships often means knowing what not to say and when not to say it. For example, maybe you did flirt harmlessly with a coworker at happy hour. If it went nowhere and meant nothing, confessing this to your partner might only inflict pain and insecurity on them for no reason. Sometimes, the *"full truth"* can feel like an emotional dump – the teller feels lighter, but the listener is now weighed down by unnecessary worry.

There's also the issue of timing. Blunt honesty delivered at the wrong moment is a recipe for disaster. Telling your spouse "I actually hate our wallpaper" during a fight about something else is not constructive – it's piling on. Announcing a long list of petty grievances or past misdeeds all at once (perhaps because you've been *"holding it in"*) can shatter your partner's trust more than if you had just kept those tidbits to yourself. Because now they're thinking: *"Have you always felt this way? What else haven't you told me?"*

Culturally, there's now an expectation of *hyper-transparency* in relationships. Sure, being open and real is good – but like oversharing on social media, oversharing in love can become performative and self-indulgent. True intimacy does not require that you both know every single thought that floats through each other's heads – that would actually be exhausting (and a little insane). Intimacy requires trust that some things can go unspoken and you'll still be understood and loved.

Take the old adage *"never go to bed angry."* Some couples take this so literally that they stay up till 3 AM analyzing every minor grievance just to avoid any secrets overnight. In reality, it's often wiser to sleep on it and talk with clear heads in the morning, instead of spilling every bean in the jar at midnight.

Bottom line: total transparency is overrated. Honesty is the best policy *when it matters*. But dumping every trivial guilt or past mistake on your partner isn't noble – it's selfish. Smart couples practice selective honesty: share the truths that matter, and let the minor secrets slide (especially if a "confession" is only to ease your own conscience).

In other words, sometimes holding your tongue is the smarter move. In the realm of pillow talk, a well-timed silence can be golden. Because at the end of the day, your relationship is not a reality TV confessional booth – it's a bond between two imperfect humans. A little tact, a little privacy, and a little faith in what doesn't need to be said can go a long way. After all, isn't it nicer to drift off on your pillows whispering *"I love you,"* rather than *"I figured I should tell you, I accidentally scratched your car three months ago'*? Some secrets are better left as dirty little secrets – and that's perfectly okay.

Chapter 4

The Ghosts of Girlfriends (and Boyfriends) Past

Picture this: It's 1 A.M., and you're illuminated by the ghostly glow of your phone screen. You *should* be asleep, but instead you're deep in a digital rabbit hole, one profile click away from finding out what your high school crush's cousin's dog had for dinner. Sound familiar? Welcome to The Ghosts of Girlfriends (and Boyfriends) Past, a haunted tour through our romantic regrets, what-ifs, and the absurd lengths we go to relive (or rewrite) the past. In this chapter, we'll confront the spirits of relationships gone by – with a wink, a nudge, and plenty of humor. Strap in for a witty, satirical romp through late-night social media stalking, the agony of *shoulda, woulda, coulda*, rose-tinted memories of exes, and the grand delusion of living with "no regrets." Spoiler: everyone has regrets (even the ones posting inspirational quotes to convince you otherwise). Now, let's dive into the fun, messy truth about love, lies, and who really left the toilet seat up.

The One That Got Away (and the Social Media Spiral)

They don't call it *the one that got away* for nothing. Maybe it was your high school sweetheart, the college crush, or that coworker you *swore* you had a moment with at the holiday party. Fast forward to tonight: you're on their LinkedIn profile, of all places, squinting at a tiny profile pic and pondering life choices. How did we end up here, deep-stalking an ex or almost-lover on social media in the wee hours? The answer is a cocktail of curiosity, nostalgia, and a dash of regret – all mixed by the capable hands of modern technology.

First off, if you've ever gone on a midnight recon mission through an ex's Instagram or a crush's Facebook, take comfort: you are very much not alone. Creeping on past flames online is practically a national pastime. One survey found that over half of Americans (about 56.5%) admit to glancing at an ex's social media at least once a month. And here's the kicker – those in relationships and even married folks are *more* likely to snoop than singles. In that poll, roughly two-thirds of married people copped to monthly ex-checks. So the next time you're clearing your browser history at 1 A.M., remember that statistically, a bunch of ostensibly happy couples are doing the exact same thing. Misery loves company, and apparently, so do curiosity and nostalgia.

But why do we do this to ourselves? Partly, it's the "digital nostalgia" factor – the internet has made it absurdly easy to relive our past, whether through Facebook Memories popping up like ghosts of timelines past or through our own late-night detective work. Unlike flipping through an old shoebox of photos, social media offers an infinite, curated museum of our lives and relationships. It's nostalgia on tap, available 24/7. Platforms like Facebook and Instagram will even *serve* you nostalgia: "On this day 10 years ago, you were blissfully posting couples selfies." Gee, thanks, Facebook, for that reminder of my peak acne years and ill-advised hairstyle. This phenomenon – where technology actively resurfaces moments from the past and amplifies our engagement with those memories – has been dubbed *digital nostalgia*. Our phones are basically time machines, and after two glasses of wine on a lonely night, we all become eager time travelers.

There's a scientific method to this memory madness. When you scroll through old posts or that crush's vacation photos, your brain actually gives you little rewards. Each time you stumble on a happy memory or see a flattering photo, your brain releases a hit of dopamine – the same feel-good chemical that rewards you for eating cake or winning at Wordle. In other words, deep-stalking your ex online is literally giving your brain mini dopamine snacks. No wonder it's *addictive*. One minute you're just checking their profile picture; the next, you're 80 weeks deep, watching a grainy video of their cousin's wedding, dopamine neurons happily buzzing. It's the modern spiral: you're not just *lost in thought*, you're lost in a meticulously documented digital archive of Someone You Used To Know.

Of course, this social media spiral tends to end in one of two ways. Best-case scenario, you satisfy your curiosity: "Ah, they *did* finally start that organic llama farm, good for them." Worst-case scenario, you accidentally tap the "Like" button on a post from 2011. (If that happens, might I suggest assuming a new identity and moving to a remote cabin immediately?) In all seriousness, late-night online stalking can stir up some emotions. You might feel a weird pang of loss seeing that *the one that got away* is now happily married with kids, or an evil spark of schadenfreude if they're, say, still posting angsty Linkin Park lyrics. Social media makes these comparisons and what-ifs inevitable. Psychologists note that having instant access to curated highlights of someone else's life can create an illusion that the past (or that person) was better than it really was, breeding a unique mix of longing and regret. It's like looking at a heavily-filtered photo – you're not seeing the whole truth, just the highlights, and suddenly your present reality feels a bit dull in comparison.

And yet, we scroll on. Why? Because the past has *pull*. That high school crush's profile becomes a portal to a simpler time; that ex's vacation pics make you reminisce about your own adventures. It's human nature to wonder *what if,* and social media is the ultimate enabler of that curiosity. Late at night, armed with a smartphone and some wistful courage, we play detective in our own love lives. Think of it as digital archaeology, digging up shards of past relationships. Sometimes you strike gold (or at least a funny old photo), and sometimes you just end up covered in the dust of memories you'd rather have left buried. Either way, it's compelling. So don't beat yourself up for the occasional 1 A.M. LinkedIn lurk-fest. It happens to the best of us. Just maybe refrain from sending any friend requests at that hour – *nothing* good ever happens on social media after midnight, except getting material for the next section of this chapter.

Shoulda, Woulda, Coulda: Missed Chances and What-Ifs

Now let's talk about those three little words that haunt every lovesick soul more than any horror movie: "shoulda, woulda, coulda." If you've ever lain awake replaying an entire alternate history in which you confessed your love to that special someone (instead of awkwardly saying "Have a nice life!" as they boarded a plane), you know this feeling. Humans have a remarkable talent for torturing ourselves with hypothetical scenarios. Romantic what-ifs are the emotional equivalent of a song stuck on repeat – incredibly hard to shake and annoyingly catchy.

Regret is a universal part of love. In fact, surveys show that romance is one of the most common sources of regret, outpacing things like education or career in many people's mental playlists of "Things I Wish I'd Done Differently." And it's not just a female thing, but women do report more of these romantic regrets than men. One study found that nearly 45% of women cited a lost love or relationship mistake as their biggest regret, compared to less than 20% of men. That's a huge gap. (The other 80% of men, for the record, were apparently busy regretting something *very important* like a missed sports game or a stock they didn't buy – priorities, right?) This isn't to say guys don't have romantic what-ifs; they absolutely do. But it seems ladies have a special aptitude for replaying those missed chances on loop. As one researcher put it, "women are the keepers of relationships" – we hold onto the memories and the could-have-beens, sometimes a little too tightly.

The funny thing about *missed chances* is how outsized they become in our minds. There's a psychological reason for this. Studies suggest that the regrets over things we *didn't do* tend to linger much longer than regrets over things we *did* (even if those things blew up in our face). The one that got away, the phone number you never dialed, the flirtation you never pursued – those "missed opportunities stick in our brains longer" and bug us more persistently than, say, that one disastrous blind date you actually went on. Basically, your brain has a harder time shutting the door on a possibility that never materialized. A bad date might make you cringe for a week, but *not asking someone out* can make you cringe for years, because your imagination keeps writing fan-fiction about what *might* have happened. As psychologist Neal Roese notes, something you did and regret will nag you immediately, but you're "more able to make peace with it" over time; whereas the path not taken is like an unfinished chapter that your mind just won't put down.

We've all been there. Maybe you still think about that friend you secretly liked but never confessed to – and now, every time you see their adorable baby photos on Facebook, you think, "That could have been *my* kid rocking the 'World's Cutest' onesie." Or maybe it's a coworker from years ago you had a spark with, but HR frowned on intra-office romance, so you played it safe. Now you're LinkedIn-stalking him (yes, back to LinkedIn – apparently the true home of unrequited love) and sighing at his professional headshot, wondering *what if*. The mind is a master storyteller, and it loves to create these elaborate alternate universes. In one, you two eloped to Fiji and have a happily-ever-after; in another, you at least got a second date and avoided the entire Tinder saga of your late twenties.

Interestingly, regret researchers have found some gender twists in the what-if department. Men, it turns out, often stew over the *women they didn't pursue.* If there's an action hero for male regret, it's the guy kicking himself for *not* kissing the girl at the party, or for *never* messaging that cute profile. Women, on the other hand, are a bit more balanced – we regret the ones we *didn't* go for and the ones we *did* (and probably shouldn't have) in almost equal measure. In other words, a guy might be haunted by the *one that got away*, while a woman might be haunted by *the one she let stay way too long.* This tracks with every rom-com ever: the male lead makes a mad dash through the airport because he can't bear the regret of not trying, whereas the female lead is often reflecting on a past relationship thinking, "Why did I stay with that jerk for five years?!" To each their own torture, right?

All these missed chances and hypothetical do-overs can be pretty amusing in hindsight. Think about it: some of the wildest what-if fantasies we have are downright absurd if we say them out loud. ("If only I had spilled coffee on *her* instead of *him*, then I'd be married to a millionaire in Paris by now!" Sure, Jan.) We humans have a knack for magical thinking when it comes to love. Every little choice feels like a sliding door that could lead to a dramatically different outcome. It's both terrifying and hilarious. Terrifying because, wow, no pressure – one mis-timed text and you might have altered your destiny. Hilarious because, come on, imagine if we actually got everything we *thought* we wanted. That high school crush you moon over might have turned out to be completely incompatible – you just didn't stick around long enough to find out. Sometimes the fantasy is better than reality ever could be.

So what do we do with this tangle of shoulda-woulda-coulda regrets? For one, we can laugh at them – gently. It's part of being human. Almost everyone has that one lingering question mark in their past. The key is not letting the ghost of a missed chance scare you out of living your life now. Sure, *in a perfect world* you would have confessed your feelings under a starlit sky, or taken that summer trip to Italy with your college crush. But in this world, you can take the lessons (always carry courage and maybe mints for impromptu kisses?) and move forward. And if the what-ifs still bug you, remember Roese's wisdom: missed opportunities nag us because we imagine they were perfect – a notion that is, frankly, *ridiculous*. The reality could have been anything from mildly disappointing to utterly disastrous. You'll never know! And maybe that's a blessing. As the saying goes, be careful what you wish for – you just might get it, and then you'd have a whole new set of regrets.

Post-Breakup Amnesia: Why Exes Look Better in Hindsight

Ah, the curious case of post-breakup amnesia. You break up with someone because, let's be honest, they drove you absolutely up the wall – perhaps they forgot your birthday *and* consistently left the toilet seat up *and* had the emotional availability of a teaspoon. At the time, you're confident it's the right call. Fast forward a few months, and you catch yourself reminiscing: "You know, maybe it wasn't that bad. Remember the way we used to slow-dance in the kitchen? And the inside jokes? Gosh, he was kind of sweet..." *Stop right there.* This is your memory playing Photoshopped tricks on you.

Our brains have a funny way of airbrushing the past, especially when it comes to exes. It's like there's an Instagram filter called "Rose-Tinted Glasses" that gets applied to all your memories without consent. Psychologists actually have a name for this phenomenon: romanticizing the past (or rosy retrospection, if you want to get fancy). We tend to remember the good times and conveniently forget the bad. As one insightful writer quipped, "It's easier to love someone when they're not there to annoy you". Ain't that the truth! Once your ex is safely out of your life, they're not around to leave socks on the floor or hog the covers, and suddenly your brain is like, "Hey, remember how they *always* brought you soup when you were sick? They were basically a saint!" Meanwhile, the memories of crying in the bathroom after that big fight start to fade like an old Polaroid.

This selective memory isn't just anecdotal – it's baked into how nostalgia works. When we get all misty-eyed about a past relationship, we're often dealing with an idealized, edited version of it. We highlight the enjoyable bits (the movie nights, the cuddles, the time you both laughed so hard you cried) and we *block out* the crappy bits (the jealousy, the awkward silences, the way they chewed with their mouth open). If our real memories were a Facebook profile, we're basically untagging all the unflattering moments. No wonder exes start to look better in hindsight – we've cropped out their flaws in our mental scrapbook.

Social media can turbocharge this effect. Think about it: if you stay Facebook or Instagram friends with an ex, what do you see? Birthday wishes, smiling photos, career achievements – a highlight reel of their life (and by extension, the slice of life you once shared). You're unlikely to see posts about the nights they were sulking or the times they made a total mess of things. In fact, social media's memory features often resurface mostly positive moments, filtering out the neutral or negative ones and making the past seem shinier than it really was. Your Facebook "On This Day" isn't going to remind you "On this day two years ago, you had a screaming match over directions to a wedding." Nope – it'll show the cute selfie from the reception where you both *looked* happy (even if you were actually arguing five minutes before). This kind of algorithmic nostalgia can distort our perception, tricking us into recalling a relationship as *80% joy* when maybe it was, in truth, 50/50 on a good day.

Beyond algorithms, our own minds play along with this con. There's something called the fading affect bias, where negative emotions fade faster than positive ones when we recall past events. It's like our brain naturally wants to let go of the pain and hold onto the warm fuzzies. Evolutionary self-care, perhaps? Great for moving on from trauma, not so great when you're trying to *stay* moved-on from an ex. Before you know it, you're reminiscing about how great your ex *looked* in that one outfit or how they *always* knew how to make you laugh – and you completely blank on the fact that, oh yeah, they also forgot to pick you up at the airport that one time. Selective amnesia at its finest.

To be fair, not all ex-remembering is bad. Nostalgia can be a healing thing in moderation. It's okay to smile at a good memory. But problems arise when you start romanticizing an ex so much that you want them back based on a fiction. We've all seen someone do this (or done it ourselves): you're lonely, you're scrolling through old photos, and suddenly you have an urge to text your ex *because in your mind they were perfect.* This is when you need a reality check. It might help to literally list out the reasons you broke up in the first place – keep that list handy like emotional smelling salts to jolt you back to sense. Your ex was (probably) not a demon, but they weren't an angel either. They were gloriously, frustratingly human – and you broke up for *valid* reasons.

If you catch yourself in a post-breakup glamour fog, do what any sensible person would: call up your brutally honest friend. You know, the one who saw the relationship without the gauzy filter. They'll be happy to remind you, *in excruciating detail,* of the time your ex ditched your birthday or how they never, ever did the dishes. Sometimes a friend's outside perspective is the reality check you need to break the spell. Another pro tip: maybe stop scrolling your ex's curated posts. It's like trying to get over a sugar addiction while living in a candy store. Give yourself some distance on social media – unfollow, mute, hide, whatever it takes. Out of sight can eventually mean (mostly) out of mind.

At the end of the day, our tendency to put exes on a pedestal from afar is just that – a tendency, not truth. Memories are malleable and often misleading. So the next time you find yourself thinking "Maybe my ex was *the best I ever had,*" remember that your mind is playing a rom-com montage, not a documentary. Every relationship has blooper reels and deleted scenes that you're conveniently not watching. Trust that there's a reason your ex is in your past, and embrace the *real* life in front of you –

messy, unfiltered, and far more authentic than any carefully cropped memory.

No Regrets (Liar, Liar)

Pop quiz: How many times have you seen someone on Instagram caption a photo with *#NoRegrets* or a quote about having no regrets in life? Too many to count, I bet. It's become a modern mantra – "No regrets!" – often accompanied by inspirational sunsets or a yoga pose. And it's about as believable as a toddler saying they didn't eat the chocolate when their face is covered in it. Let's be real: *everyone* has regrets, especially in the romance department. Claiming otherwise is like claiming you've never passed gas – we know you're full of hot air.

Why are we so obsessed with appearing regret-free? Perhaps it's aspirational; it sounds cool and brave to say "I regret nothing!" It's the kind of self-deception we applaud on social media. But let's call it out: "no regrets" is a lie – a well-intentioned, life-affirming lie – but a lie nonetheless. Those quote-posting, positivity-preaching people have as many romantic facepalm moments as the rest of us. The difference is, they've slapped a faux-enlightened filter on them. Did you *really* need to drunk-text your ex "U up? I missss u" that one time? Regret level: high. What about that rebound fling with the walking red flag you dated just to prove you were over your breakup? Yep, regret. Or the soulmate who was in front of you all along, but you were too busy playing games to realize it – big regret. We've got them all: the regrettable rebound, the unsent (or worse, sent) texts, the missed hints, the accidental insults, the one that got away, the one that should've gotten away sooner. Congratulations, you're human.

Ironically, owning our regrets can be kind of liberating. There's a kernel of truth in those cheesy quotes: every regret *does* teach you something, even if it's just "never mix tequila and Tinder." A renowned psychologist, Neal Roese, even points out that regret has an upside – it helps us put things in perspective and recognize what we truly value. In the realm of romance, that means those cringey moments and soulful sighs can actually guide you toward better choices. Think of regret as the relationship autopsy report: it tells you cause of death, so your next love has a better chance of survival. Maybe you regret not apologizing to an ex – now you learn the importance of pride-swallowing. Maybe you regret *settling* for less than you deserved – now you're holding out for the real thing. In a twisted way, regrets are our wise (if slightly sarcastic) mentors.

Let's also appreciate the comedic side of our romantic regrets. With enough time, many of them turn into hilarious anecdotes. The awful date you regret going on becomes the funny story you tell at parties. The ex you regret dumping (or not dumping sooner) becomes a character in your personal sitcom, complete with catchphrases. Sometimes you have to laugh at the fact that you once thought texting a Shakespearean sonnet to your unrequited crush was a good idea (regret and cringe, table for one!). Humor is how we heal. By laughing at our past follies, we take their power away. It's like saying, "Yeah, I did that, it was dumb, but hey – I lived to joke about it."

Still, it's worth poking fun at the whole *#NoRegrets culture*. All those posts about living with zero regrets gloss over an important truth: Regret is not only normal, it's downright inevitable in love. You *will* sometimes wish you had done things differently. And that's okay! It doesn't mean you're failing at life; it means you care enough to reflect. The goal shouldn't be to have *no* regrets – it should be not letting regrets *consume* you or define you. Big difference. One is unattainable perfection; the other is healthy introspection.

If you ask me, a more honest hashtag would be #LearnedAndLaughing. Because that's what we do: we learn from the loves that didn't last, and we (eventually) laugh at the embarrassing stuff. Your exes, your almost-loves, your could-have-beens – they're all part of your story, and yes, some chapters are cringe comedy. Own it. Even the superstar celebs posting cryptic "no regrets" quotes have diaries full of "oops" in the romance section. Trust me.

So the next time you scroll past a glossy post declaring "live life with no regrets" and you feel a twinge because, well, you *do* have some – maybe a lot – just smile. That quote is an aspiration, not a reality. Real life is messy. Real love is messier. We all occasionally wish we could ghostbuster the ghosts of girlfriends and boyfriends past – or at least give them a stern talking-to about the emotional havoc they wreak. But those ghosts, those memories and lessons, are part of who we are. Regrets and all.

In the end, here's the messy truth: love and regret are two sides of the same coin. You can't truly have one without the possibility of the other. Every time you risk your heart, you risk a future "what was I thinking?!" moment. And that's okay. It's worth it. Because amidst the confessions, the regrets, and the affairs of the heart (yes, even the ones involving toilet seats up), we find growth, humor, and humanity. We learn to stalk a little less, to seize the moment a little more, to remember things as they *were*, not as our nostalgia paints them, and to embrace our regrets as proof that we *tried*.

So here's to the ghosts of relationships past – may we acknowledge them, learn from them, have a good laugh about them, and then politely ask them to leave us alone... at least until the next 1 A.M. social media spiral. Cheers, and *no regrets* – well, maybe just a few, and that's perfectly okay.

Chapter 5

The Affair and the Fury – Cheaters, Lies, and Alibis

The Cheat Sheet: Why Good People Stray

Let's start with a jaw-dropping truth: many people who cheat *still* love their partners. Yes, you read that right. In one extensive survey of straying spouses, a whopping 88.7% of men and 71.1% of women reported that they "still loved" their spouse even during the affair. It seems you can break vows and hearts yet *still* have warm fuzzies for the person you're betraying – human beings are *nothing* if not complicated. So the usual villain-vs-victim narrative? Not so simple. Often, infidelity isn't about a lack of love; it's about a lack of *something else*. Many cheaters aren't out to discard their partners like last season's fashion – they're seeking the missing spark, the lost thrill, or just a solution to terminal bedroom boredom while still wearing the "loving spouse" T-shirt.

Why do happy-ish people stray? Research shows a buffet of motivating factors beyond the cartoonish "evil cheater" trope. A University of Maryland study identified eight common reasons people cheat, and none of them was "because I'm just a terrible person". Some did it out of anger or revenge, others cited neglect – not getting enough attention or respect at home. Plenty were seeking sexual variety or novel experiences, even while still being in love with their partner. In plainer terms: they're bored or sexually unsatisfied, not necessarily devoid of love or conscience. As one of the researchers put it, infidelity can happen "even [to] couples in seemingly stable relationships," and many reasons for cheating "are not a direct reflection of a relationship's health.". In other words, even "good" people in good relationships might wander, not because their partner is awful, but because humans have an uncanny ability to get restless and curious (or make colossally poor decisions) despite themselves.

This perspective turns the typical blame game on its head. It's often said that an affair is a symptom of a broken relationship, but reality isn't so black-and-white. *"Our research suggests it's not that simple: People cheat for a variety of reasons, many of which are not a direct reflection of a relationship's health,"* notes psychologist Dylan Selterman. Maybe the cheater is feeling unappreciated or unloved (neglect), or just craving the thrill of something new after 20 years of Meatloaf Mondays (variety). Sometimes it's pure sexual desire – the person loves their spouse *but* really misses swinging from the chandeliers, if you catch my drift. In other cases, it's situational: the stars (and maybe some tequila shots) aligned to create a perfect storm of poor judgment (think business trip + hotel bar + zero supervision). We also can't forget esteem – the clichéd midlife crisis affair where someone seeks validation that they've "still got it" by seducing a new fling 20 years their junior. None of these reasons excuse the lies, of course, but they sure explain why infidelity is exceedingly common across cultures and eras.

Indeed, infidelity is *so common* it's almost ordinary – which is both comforting and disturbing. By some estimates, roughly 20% of married men and 13% of married women in the U.S. have cheated on their spouse, and that's just those willing to admit it in surveys. The reality is likely higher. Affairs happen in humble homes and Hollywood mansions alike. They happen not necessarily because every cheater is a heartless jerk, but often because even basically decent people find themselves unsatisfied, bored, or emotionally disconnected in monogamy and make really bad choices in response. The old rhyme *"if you can't be with the one you love, love the one you're with"* occasionally gets twisted into "love the one you're with, but also hook up with the one you *shouldn't.*"

So, why do good people stray? The answers are messy: because humans get lonely, or curious, or insecure; because passion can fade and temptation is everywhere; because life is long and our attention spans are short. It's not *just* a tale of predators and victims. It can be the tale of someone who genuinely adores their spouse yet yearns for excitement or affirmation. As paradoxical as it sounds, a serial cheater might still come home every night, say "I love you," and mean it – right before sending a few spicy texts to a secret lover. Infidelity lives in that gray zone of love and lust, routine and adventure. It's a place where you can sincerely cherish your partner *and* deceive them in the next breath. If that makes your head spin, welcome to the wild contradictions of the human heart.

Before we grab our pitchforks, this isn't about justifying cheating – it's about understanding it. A more nuanced view shows that infidelity isn't always the final verdict on a relationship's value. Some affairs truly are one-off mistakes by people who were otherwise devoted; other times, they signal deeper issues or unmet needs that the couple ignored for too long. Boredom, for instance, is a quiet killer – plenty of unfaithful partners report that the spark had dimmed and routine suffocated the romance, even though they still *loved* their partner deeply. One recent study of active cheaters (on the infamous site Ashley Madison, no less) found exactly this pattern: participants reported very high love for their spouses but very low sexual satisfaction. In fact, sexual dissatisfaction was the primary motivator to cheat, rather than big relationship problems. They weren't out to replace their spouse; they were out to replace their Netflix-and-chill rut with something…hotter.

It's an uncomfortable truth that "good" people – loving parents, caring spouses, pillars of the community – might stray given the right (or wrong) circumstances. The suburban dad who coaches soccer might also have a Tinder alias. The devoted wife who volunteers at the school might be having a fling with her coworker over lunch breaks. It's not necessarily because they've turned into villains overnight. Often, it's because they felt lonely in the marriage, or unappreciated, or just emotionally numb and seeking a jolt. In a culture that loves clear heroes and villains, this is the jaw-dropping twist: sometimes the cheater *and* the cheated-on can both be sympathetic figures. Affairs hurt, *no doubt*, but the people in them might not fit neatly into sinner vs. saint. It's more like lost vs. lost-er.

So, why do good people cheat? To sum up the cheat sheet (pun intended):

- **They're bored or craving excitement.** Still love their partner, but miss the *zing!* in their lives. (Monogamy, it turns out, can get monotonous.)

- **They feel neglected or unappreciated.** An affair can become an ego booster or a source of the attention they lack at home.

- **They're sexually unsatisfied.** Instead of communicating about spicing up the marriage, they seek satisfaction on the side. (Spoiler: this usually ends badly for all involved.)

- **It was situational or impulsive.** Right place, wrong time (or wrong state of inebriation). Sometimes a "good" person does a *very* bad thing once, almost by accident – and instantly regrets it (or so they claim).

- **They seek emotional connection.** Surprisingly, some affairs are more about feelings than sex. A person might feel a soulmate-level bond with someone new while still loving their spouse – a mind-bending situation that fuels many a soap opera subplot.

In the end, infidelity is a realm of contradictions. Love and betrayal coexist uneasily. The cheater isn't always a cold-hearted scoundrel, and the faithful partner isn't always an angel (though they certainly don't deserve the hurt). Understanding this doesn't excuse lying and sneaking around, but it does bust the myth that only "bad people" cheat. Sometimes wonderful, kind, *ordinary* people blow up their own lives – and the lives of those they love – in moments of weakness or desire. It's equal parts tragic, fascinating, and darkly human. And it's exactly why stories of affairs have captivated us for centuries. Speaking of which, let's talk about some of those stories – the scandals that rocked worlds and made headlines, proving that when it comes to cheating, truth is stranger (and juicier) than fiction.

The Distracted Boyfriend Effect

Picture that viral meme: A guy walks with his girlfriend but turns his head, ogling a beautiful stranger passing by, while his girlfriend shoots daggers from her eyes. You know the one – the "Distracted Boyfriend" meme. It became an internet sensation precisely *because* it was so relatable and funny; in one snapshot, it captured the timeless human condition of temptation. (Fun fact: the photographer who shot that stock photo *intentionally* set out to represent infidelity "in a playful and fun way" – mission accomplished!). The meme morphed into jokes about everything from procrastination to political betrayals, but at its core is that universal scenario: being in a committed relationship yet momentarily bewitched by the *"Oooh, shiny!"* allure of someone new. Let's call it the Distracted Boyfriend Effect – a perfect metaphor for why staying monogamous can feel like trying to focus on salad when a pizza is waving at you from across the room.

Modern life offers an endless parade of potential distractions. That "boyfriend" in the meme? He's basically all of us in the age of Instagram and dating apps – commitment in one hand, curiosity in the other. Monogamy, wonderful as it can be, is challenging even in satisfactory relationships. It's like committing to eat only your favorite meal every day while living in a food court; sooner or later, the aroma of pepperoni or

Pad Thai might turn your head. Research backs this up in rather startling ways. In a 2023 study of nearly 2,000 active cheaters (yes, researchers bravely went there), people admitted that even though they *loved* their spouses, they found monogamy hard and their affairs highly satisfying. In fact, the study reported "maintaining monogamy is challenging" for most folks, and novelty and excitement – the very stuff depicted by that wandering-eye meme – were driving many to cheat. Think of monogamy as walking a straight line: it's not impossible, but wow, are there a lot of interesting side paths and billboards vying for your attention.

What about guilt, you ask? Shouldn't that wandering boyfriend feel bad? Pop culture would have us think that every cheater is tormented by remorse – wringing their hands, delivering tearful confessions, etc. But reality paints a different (and rather unnerving) picture. That same survey of cheaters found that the majority did *not* regret their affairs and in fact rated them as highly satisfying both sexually and emotionally. Read that again and let it sink in: a lot of real-life "distracted boyfriends (and girlfriends)" are apparently quite content with their extracurricular activities. One infidelity researcher noted how movies and books portray cheating lovers as racked with guilt, but "we don't see that in this sample" – instead, satisfaction was high and feelings of regret were low. In other words, the meme guy checking out another girl isn't losing sleep; he's probably sleeping *soundly*, dreaming of his next rendezvous, while his poor girlfriend is left fuming.

This lack of remorse among cheaters is a serious reality check. We often assume a cheater must be either heartless or else guilt-ridden and seeking redemption. Turns out, many are neither – they compartmentalize like pros. They genuinely believe (or rationalize) that a little side fling won't "harm their marriage", especially if the spouse never finds out. Hence the classic cheater's mantra: *"What they don't know won't hurt them."* The Distracted Boyfriend Effect in real life is bolstered by a curious blend of entitlement and optimism – *I deserve this fun; I can have it all; no one gets hurt.* It's the same energy as sneaking a cookie from the jar and thinking as long as you don't get caught, no calories count.

Let's not forget the role of modern technology in amplifying temptation. Our meme boyfriend only had one attractive stranger crossing his path; today's would-be cheater has thousands of attractive strangers crossing their screen daily. One swipe on a dating app or a flirtatious DM on Instagram can instantly connect a bored partner with a new *object of interest*. It's like an all-you-can-eat buffet of distraction, available 24/7. No wonder fidelity feels like a Herculean task for some. Maintaining focus on one person romantically requires not just love, but active effort and sometimes blinders to avoid the daily parade of alternatives. Evolutionary psychology even argues that humans aren't naturally wired for strict monogamy – historically, many cultures accepted multiple lovers, concubines, etc., so perhaps our instincts lag behind our ideals.

But before we give every cheater a free pass (*"biology made me do it!"*), let's inject some personal responsibility. The Distracted Boyfriend Effect is an explanation, not an excuse. Yes, temptation is everywhere, and yes, monogamy can feel like dieting in a candy store. But plenty of people still manage to stay faithful by exercising a muscle called self-control (and perhaps not placing themselves in situations ripe for infidelity – pro tip: if you don't want to slip, don't hang out at the skating rink of temptation!). The meme might be funny, but in real life, being on the receiving end of that meme (as the ignored girlfriend) is painful and humiliating.

What's fascinating is how *little* remorse some cheaters report in studies – a fact that shocks the faithful and validates the cynics. Cheaters often describe their affairs in almost refreshing terms: fulfilling needs that weren't met, adding excitement to life, even making them *happier* at home because their itch was scratched elsewhere. Twisted logic? Absolutely. But it's a logic that exists. One cheater might say, "Honestly, the affair made me more cheerful around my spouse because I wasn't frustrated anymore." Yikes. It's the have-your-cake-and-eat-it-too mentality, set to a smooth R&B soundtrack.

The Distracted Boyfriend meme's enduring popularity hints at another uncomfortable truth: a lot of people *identify* with it, on one side or the other. Either you've been the guy sneaking a peek, or you fear your partner doing the sneaking. It taps into a collective anxiety about loyalty in an age of infinite options. The meme is humorous because it's exaggerated – the guy turning his whole head in broad daylight – but also because it's relatable. Who hasn't noticed an attractive stranger even while with someone you love? The gap between noticing and acting is where character comes in. Most of us notice; far fewer actually pursue.

But those who do pursue often don't turn back – at least not until they're caught.

To sum up the Distracted Boyfriend Effect: temptation is everywhere, monogamy is hard, and modern cheaters often shockingly lack guilt. The boyfriend in the meme might feel a twinge of shame when his girlfriend glares, but in real life many cheaters just carry on, managing their double lives with minimal remorse. It's a sobering thought that challenges the narratives of cheaters as either monstrous or repentant. Many are neither; they're simply *distracted* – and quite enjoying the view. In the grand circus of infidelity, temptation is the ringleader, and remorse is the sad clown who sometimes doesn't show up at all.

Now that we've explored *why* people stray and how temptation seduces, it's time for some juicy tales. Buckle up for a whirlwind tour of the most infamous affairs and scandals – the ones that made history, spawned memes (or would have, if Twitter existed in the 16th century), and left a trail of lies, tears, and occasionally, very awkward press conferences.

Scandals and Consequences

Throughout history, nothing sparks gossip (and moral outrage) quite like a good affair scandal. From kings and queens to presidents, preachers, and pop stars, the world has been *both* horrified and titillated by tales of illicit love. In this section, we'll take a witty, whirlwind tour of some of the most infamous affairs ever – complete with secret love letters, public apologies, and tabloid disasters that left reputations in tatters. Consider this the highlight reel of humanity's longest-running reality show: Cheaters, Lies, and Alibis. *Cue the dramatic music and popcorn.*

- **King Henry VIII & Anne Boleyn (1520s):** Let's start with a royal doozy. King Henry VIII of England didn't just cheat – he changed the course of history for his mistress. Bored with wife #1, Henry became besotted with the witty Anne Boleyn and embarked on an affair that led him to defy the Pope, dump Queen Catherine, and launch the English Reformation (when cheating causes a whole new church to form, you know it's big). In the meantime, Henry bombarded Anne with steamy love letters – 17 of them survive, now kept in the Vatican library, reportedly stolen by agents of the Pope as "evidence" of Henry's infidelity. These handwritten 16th-century sexts reveal a king utterly lovesick ("my heart and I surrender unto you," he cooed in one). Talk about secret letters – Henry's passionate missives to Anne were essentially the *Tudor-era equivalent of late-night texts*. The affair-turned-marriage didn't end well (Anne lost her head – literally – after Henry accused her of treason and adultery, oh the irony), but their scandalous liaison remains legendary. When a king's wandering eye leads to excommunication and internal church memos, you've got a scandal for the ages.

- **John F. Kennedy & Marilyn Monroe (1960s):** Fast forward to a mash-up of Hollywood glamour and political power. President JFK was *allegedly* a prolific womanizer (Secret Service code name: "Lothario-in-Chief"... okay, we made that up). Of all his rumored flings, none is more famous than Marilyn Monroe. The iconic blonde bombshell and the dashing young president – it sounds like fan fiction, yet evidence suggests it happened. Rumors had swirled for years, but the affair legend peaked when Marilyn breathily cooed *"Happy Birthday, Mr. President"* in a skintight gown at JFK's 45th birthday gala in 1962. That sultry public serenade all but confirmed to the world that something scandalous was up. (First Lady Jackie Kennedy's absence from that event was notable – perhaps she didn't care to watch her husband's rumored mistress sing to him in front of a live audience.) It's said Marilyn and JFK had a brief tryst or two, and possibly an entanglement with JFK's brother Bobby as well. The details remain murky (no stained dress to DNA-test in this case), but the cultural impact is clear: the image of Marilyn, Hollywood's brightest star, tangled in a *"scandalous affair"* with the president has been immortalized in countless books and conspiracy theories. It's the ultimate tale of glitz, power, and tragic consequences – weeks after JFK ended things, Marilyn died under mysterious circumstances, fueling endless speculation that the affair fallout played a part. We'll never fully know, but one thing's certain: Monroe and Kennedy's alleged liaison still captivates and scandalizes, a symbol of the dangerous liaison between celebrity and politics.

- **Bill Clinton & Monica Lewinsky (1990s):** "I did not have sexual relations with that woman, Miss Lewinsky." – With that single sentence in January 1998, delivered on national TV with a pointed finger for emphasis, President Bill Clinton etched himself into the scandal hall of fame. Spoiler: he *did* have sexual relations with that woman, a 22-year-old White House intern, and the attempted cover-up nearly toppled his presidency. This affair had everything: secret encounters in the Oval Office, a betrayed First Lady steadfastly standing by him, an incriminating blue dress with DNA evidence, and a zealous independent prosecutor turning a personal indiscretion into a federal case. When the story broke, the Clintons went into damage control overdrive. Bill's famous denial (now a meme-worthy soundbite) was followed by months of political drama culminating in him becoming the first sitting U.S. President to be impeached over personal misconduct. The scandal introduced the world to the cringe-worthy specifics of cigars and phone sex transcripts – late-night comedians had a field day. And poor Monica Lewinsky became the unfair poster child for "other woman" shaming in the internet age. In the end, Clinton survived the impeachment trial and finished his term, but not before delivering a public apology of sorts: *"Indeed, I did have a relationship with Ms. Lewinsky that was not appropriate,"* he admitted in August '98, looking suitably chagrined on camera. The consequences? A tarnished legacy, a new entry in every history textbook, and a permanent national lesson in what not to do with interns. If ever there was an affair that proved the cover-up is worse than the crime, this was it. Also, a linguistic legacy: many Americans learned creative new definitions of what does or doesn't count as "sexual relations." (Clinton's answer: apparently not oral sex – a distinction that baffled and amused the public in equal measure.)

- **Prince Charles, Princess Diana & Camilla Parker Bowles (1980s–90s):** Even the staid British monarchy couldn't avoid a royal love triangle of soap-opera proportions. Prince Charles married the beloved Lady Diana in a fairy-tale wedding in 1981, but behind palace doors, he never got over his old flame, Camilla. The affair between Charles and Camilla simmered through the '80s, with Diana gradually realizing she had a "third person" in her marriage – as she famously told a BBC interviewer, *"there were three of us in this marriage, so it was a bit crowded."* The scandal truly exploded in the early '90s with "Camillagate", a leaked 1989 phone recording so embarrassingly intimate it made the nation spit out its tea. In this not-so-sexy "sexting" of its day, Charles murmured he wished he could live in Camilla's trousers – or even be her tampon (yes, he went *there*, and yes, the tabloids printed every cringey word). Britain was scandalized; late-night hosts had a ball. The fallout? Charles and Diana separated, then divorced in 1996, with Diana dropping quotable bombs about everyone involved. Tragically, Diana died in a car crash a year later, cementing her status as "People's Princess" and casting Charles and Camilla as history's villains in many eyes. Yet time (and royal PR) heals some wounds: Charles eventually married Camilla in 2005. She's now Queen Consort, proof that sometimes the mistress *does* become the wife – though at the cost of decades of public ire. The Charles-Diana-Camilla saga remains one of the

20th century's most scandalous affairs, involving taped calls, tell-all books, and a public relations nightmare for the House of Windsor. It showed that even princes can be "distracted boyfriends," and even princesses can reach a breaking point.

- **Governor Mark Sanford & the "Appalachian Trail" (2009):** Not all cheating scandals are glitz and glamour – some are delightfully absurd. Mark Sanford, then governor of South Carolina, provided late-night comedy gold when he literally disappeared from his state for six days in June 2009. His staff sheepishly told reporters the governor was "hiking the Appalachian Trail." That turned out to be *code* for "canoodling in Argentina." Sanford had secretly flown to Buenos Aires to visit his mistress, an Argentine journalist, while everyone back home frantically wondered if their governor had fallen off a mountain or been abducted by aliens. When caught, Sanford delivered a rambling, tearful press conference in which he confessed to the affair (calling his mistress his "soul mate" – oof) and apologized to pretty much everyone, including his scorned wife Jenny. The term "hiking the Appalachian Trail" instantly became a cheeky euphemism for sneaking off to cheat. The *consequences* for Sanford were swift: he was censured by the state legislature and resigned as head of the Republican Governors Association. His marriage imploded (Jenny Sanford famously refused to stand by him like some political wives do). Amazingly, Mark Sanford's story didn't end there – in a tale of post-scandal resurrection, he later won a seat in Congress (because apparently voters in South Carolina can forgive a little international adultery if you lay on enough Southern charm). Still, his affair is forever enshrined in scandal lore thanks to that ridiculous hiking cover story. Pro-tip: if you're going to lie about your whereabouts, maybe don't choose a famous U.S. trail that journalists can quickly verify you *didn't* actually hike.

■ **Tiger Woods & the Bunker Full of Mistresses (2009):** Even by celebrity standards, Tiger Woods' fall from grace was epic. The greatest golfer in the world turned out to be a prolific cheater off the course, with a roster of mistresses so long it could fill a PGA tournament. It all came crashing down one Thanksgiving night when Tiger's enraged wife, Elin, reportedly chased him with a golf club (talk about *iron*-y) after discovering his infidelities, causing Tiger to crash his SUV into a fire hydrant. In the ensuing weeks, more than a dozen women – nightclub hostesses, porn stars, you name it – came forward claiming affairs with Tiger. The squeaky-clean icon's image was shattered. Companies pulled endorsements faster than you can say "infidelity clause." Facing a public relations nightmare, Tiger did the only thing possible: a nationally televised apology straight out of the crisis management handbook. Looking somber and robotic, he admitted the truth: *"I was unfaithful. I had affairs. I cheated,"* Woods said in a 2010 press conference, adding, *"What I did was not acceptable."*. It was a carefully scripted mea culpa, with Tiger alternately staring at the camera and the floor, acknowledging how his selfish behavior hurt his family. He announced a hiatus from golf to attend therapy and "find himself." The public reaction was mixed – some sympathized with his admission of sex addiction, others rolled their eyes at the canned apologies. The consequences were severe: a divorce that reportedly cost him over $100 million, lost sponsorships, and a tarnished legacy (at least for a while). It took years for Tiger to climb back both in golf and public esteem, showing that even the mightiest superstar isn't immune to scandal. If nothing else, Tiger Woods' saga gave us a textbook example of the modern public apology tour, and a reminder that a pristine public image can hide a very messy private life. Plus, late-night comics will *never* run out of golf puns for cheating after this ("Tiger's biggest handicap was his zipper," etc.).

- **François Mitterrand's Double Life (1980s–90s):** Affaires de cœur aren't limited to the Anglosphere. French President François Mitterrand carried on a *decades-long* secret affair during his 14 years in power – and managed to keep it mostly hidden until the very end. Mitterrand had a mistress, Anne Pingeot, and together they had a daughter, Mazarine, whose existence was kept under wraps from the public for years. It was something of an open secret among French elites and journalists, who (in that oh-so-French way) chose to respect the president's private life… until a magazine cover in 1994 blew it open with a paparazzi photo of Mitterrand and his 20-year-old love child dining together. The French reaction? A collective Gallic shrug and a muttered *"C'est la vie."* The real spectacle came in January 1996, when Mitterrand died. At his funeral, the worlds collided:

Mitterrand's *legitimate* family – his wife Danielle and their sons – walked side by side in mourning with his *illegitimate* family – Anne and daughter Mazarine. The widow even invited the mistress to stand with them, and at one point publicly embraced young Mazarine, an image that astonished viewers and was broadcast globally. Imagine the scene: a solemn state funeral with world leaders in attendance, and front and center, the wife on one arm and the mistress on the other. It was the most French resolution to an affair scandal ever – tragic, poetic, and oddly civilized. Danielle Mitterrand later coolly stated, *"Francois was my husband, and Mazarine is his daughter. That's that."* Try to picture an American president's wife saying that! The Mitterrand affair, rather than causing tabloid hysteria (though there was some), mostly prompted philosophical debates in France about privacy and the *ménage à trois* nature of power. To this day, it's cited as an example of France's relaxed attitude toward leaders' infidelities – and it stands as a scandal where the *consequences* were minimal professionally (he remained in office), but personally profound in the most public way.

Those are just a sampling – the highlight reel – of global affair scandals. There are countless more: Princess Caroline Matilda and Johann Struensee (18th-century Danish queen and her doctor, leading to a coup!), Emperor Napoleon and Josephine (he cheated incessantly; she probably did too – drama ensued), celebrity bust-ups like Brad Pitt, Jennifer Aniston & Angelina Jolie (Hollywood's millennial love triangle that launched a million gossip mags), Governor Eliot Spitzer (a crusading NY governor caught seeing high-priced escorts, who resigned in disgrace), and even televangelist scandals like Jimmy Swaggart (the preacher caught with a prostitute, weeping "I have sinned!" on TV). In each case, the pattern is familiar: secret passion, sensational reveal, public outrage, *and* often a highly choreographed apology or downfall. The consequences vary – some careers implode, some marriages end, some reputations rebound over time (Americans love a comeback story). But the *stories* themselves? They live on, fueling novels, movies, and our collective fascination. We are drawn to these scandals not just for the salacious details (though let's be honest, who isn't at least *a little* curious about a leaked love letter or a secretly recorded call?), but because they're human dramas writ large. They show powerful or famous people brought low by the same impulses that plague mere mortals. Cheaters – they're just like us (only with more cameras watching)!

In each of these affairs, you find the classic elements: lies told and exposed, alibis concocted and debunked, tearful press conferences or royal decrees, the works. There are often *letters* or nowadays texts/emails that surface (the receipts!), embarrassing recordings or photos (thank you, paparazzi and hackers), and the inevitable spectacle of a public figure saying sorry (or vehemently denying until they can't). From Henry VIII's quill-written love letters to Tiger Woods' televised apology with sound bites for the ages, the mediums change but the message is the same: illicit passion leaves a paper trail and public humiliation in its wake.

And let's spare a thought for the *other* parties in these sagas – the betrayed spouses. History and pop culture have given us a gallery of stoic figures standing by in public (hello, Hillary Clinton at that infamous 1998 press conference), or going full fury (hello, Bernadine in *Waiting to Exhale*, torching her cheating husband's car). For every scandal, there's often a scorned partner who becomes a character in the drama, eliciting public sympathy or scorn (sometimes unfairly – remember how Silda Spitzer was criticized for looking like a prop next to her contrite husband?). Some, like Diana, break their silence and spin their own narrative; others, like Elin Nordegren (Tiger's ex), take a baseball bat to a Cadillac and then take a hefty divorce settlement to start fresh. Each scandal leaves a trail of personal wreckage even as the public devours the story.

The cultural impact of these affairs is huge. They change how we talk about sex, power, and trust. Clinton and Lewinsky's saga arguably shifted American attitudes towards privacy and what counts as "impeachable" (turns out, most agreed a consensual affair, however tawdry, didn't justify removal from office). The Charles-Diana affair fundamentally altered the British royal family's image and paved the way (decades later) for a more modern monarchy (Charles *did* eventually get to publicly love the woman he always loved – but at great cost). And every celebrity affair from the Pitt-Jolie-Aniston triangle to Beyoncé and Jay-Z (more on them soon) sparks conversations about why people cheat, whether relationships can survive it, and the double standards in how male vs. female cheaters are judged in society.

Scandals also serve as cautionary tales – they put the consequences of cheating on full display for all to see. Careers ended in shame, families torn apart, public reputations permanently scarred. Yet, intriguingly, some people see these very consequences and still roll the dice in their own lives, convinced they won't get caught or their situation is "different." Spoiler: it usually isn't. If kings, presidents, and A-list celebrities – with all their resources and image managers – can't escape the fallout, chances are *you* won't either, Mr. or Ms. Cheater reading this (not that *you*, dear reader, would ever… we're speaking hypothetically, of course).

By now, we've seen the affair playbook: *Desire. Deception. Discovery. Disaster.* Maybe some attempts at damage control mixed in. But what about *after* the disaster? Can there be redemption, forgiveness – a second act to these dramas? Grab a fresh cup of tea (or wine, no judgment) and read on, because the aftermath is a whole saga unto itself.

Forgive and Forget? (The Aftermath)

So the affair is out in the open – cue the screaming, crying, lawyers dialing in, and maybe a vase or two flying across the room. What happens *after* the betrayal bomb drops? Is it possible to forgive and move forward, or is the relationship doomed to join the Titanic at the bottom of the ocean? The aftermath of infidelity is, in a word, messy. It can involve anything from heartfelt reconciliation and years of therapy to scorched-earth divorces and custody battles worthy of a soap opera. In this section, we'll explore that wild post-affair landscape with dark humor and a dash of hope, looking at how some famous couples navigated (or failed to navigate) the road to forgiveness.

First off, let's acknowledge the obvious: not everyone deals with infidelity the same way. Some shout *"Off with their head!"* (figuratively... usually) and call the divorce attorney before the cheater can even say "I'm sorry." Others grit their teeth, decide to work it out, and enter the long, winding tunnel of rebuilding trust. What factors predict who reconciles and who splits? Interestingly, research suggests a bit of a double standard at play. One large survey found that men who cheated were far more likely to reconcile with their partners than women who cheated – about 84.6% of male cheaters stayed or got back together with their original partner, compared to only 68.0% of female cheaters who did. In plain English, wives are apparently more inclined to forgive husbands for straying than vice versa. When the *wife* is the one who had the affair, husbands are less likely to stick around. This might reflect societal norms (the old "men cheat for sex, women cheat for love" stereotype making male pride less able to handle wifey's infidelity), or simply different personal boundaries. Either way, it's a statistic that screams *double standard*. A cheating husband might find his wife willing to attempt counseling; a cheating wife might find her husband already on Zillow looking for bachelor pads. Forgiveness, it seems, is not dealt out equally.

Now, let's talk therapy. Lots and lots of therapy. After the affair, if a couple chooses to stay together, they often enter a period that's equal parts awkward, painful, and hopeful – kind of like adolescence, but with more crying in parked cars. Therapists' offices fill up with pairs of red-eyed partners dissecting what went wrong. Rebuilding trust is a slow grind: the betrayed partner oscillates between anger and cautious optimism; the unfaithful partner must display saint-like transparency and patience. There are apologies – not the quick "sorry" kind, but the deeply reflective, repeated kind. As Tiger Woods put it (after a considerable nudge from PR coaches), *"My real apology to [my wife] will not come in the form of words; it will come from my behavior over time."* In other words, *show* you're sorry by being an open book and model spouse henceforth, because words are cheap when you've been caught with your pants down (literally).

Some couples emerge from this gauntlet stronger (or so they claim). They often say the affair was a wake-up call that forced them to address long-festering issues. A few even preach that it saved their marriage in a twisted way – though most betrayed folks would probably trade that "growth opportunity" for not having been cheated on, thanks. Still, notable examples of reconciliation exist. Beyoncé and Jay-Z are a prime contemporary case. When Jay-Z's infidelity came to light (remember the infamous 2014 elevator video of Beyoncé's sister Solange going all ninja on Jay-Z? That was our first big clue something was amiss), the power couple didn't split. Instead, they went to therapy and turned their marital strife into platinum art. Beyoncé's acclaimed 2016 album *Lemonade* laid bare her pain and anger (in poetic lyrics and stunning visuals), essentially announcing, *"Boy, you broke my heart, and I am not okay right now."* A year later, Jay-Z released *4:44*, essentially his musical apology and reflection on how he nearly "lost the one" because of his ego and issues. In interviews, Jay-Z admitted they chose to fight for their marriage: *"Most people walk away... The hardest thing is seeing pain on someone's face that you caused,"* he said, acknowledging that facing himself and not losing his family was the tougher path. It's almost romantic in a twisted way – they used *music as couples' therapy,* sharing their journey with millions. And guess what? They're still together, seemingly happier than ever, having added a set of twins to their brood. It's a high-profile testament that forgiveness is possible, though it likely required Beyoncé-sized strength (and a reputed list of strict post-cheating rules Jay must follow, according to gossip rags). The takeaway: if Queen Bey can forgive and even collab on a joint album with her formerly wayward hubby, maybe there's hope for mere mortals.

Another famous example: Bill and Hillary Clinton. After the Lewinsky scandal, many predicted the Clintons' marriage was toast once Bill left office. Yet, they're still together decades later. Hillary wrote in her memoir that forgiveness was a long, painful process, but she chose to stay because she still loved him and valued the life they built. Cynics say it was political convenience; Hillary counters that it was personal. Regardless, their partnership endured one of the most public betrayals ever. They did couples counseling, spiritual counseling – you name it – and somehow arrived at a détente. While opinions vary on the health of their marriage, it stands as an example that not every betrayed wife (or husband) walks away. Some dig in their heels and say, *"We'll get through this."* In Hillary's case, maybe add a mental note: *"And I'll have my turn being President, thank you very much."* (Though that second part didn't quite pan out, sadly.)

Of course, for every Jay & Bey or Bill & Hill, there's a dozen celeb couples that imploded from infidelity. Tiger Woods' marriage did not survive his scandal — Elin Nordegren took the kids and the colossal settlement and never looked back (aside from wielding that golf club of justice). Sandra Bullock & Jesse James? Split. Eva Longoria & Tony Parker? Divorced after his sexting came to light. Arnold Schwarzenegger & Maria Shriver? Terminated — learning your husband fathered a child with the housekeeper will do that. And sometimes, even if a couple *stays* officially married, the relationship is never quite the same. There can be a lingering unease, a loss of that innocent trust. The phrase "forgive and forget" is a bit misleading — you might forgive (in time), but few people genuinely *forget*. It becomes a chapter in your story, one that can be referenced in every future argument with a deft, "Oh, you took out the trash? Great. Remember that time you slept with my best friend? Just checking." (Not exactly healthy, but entirely human.)

Pop culture often reflects these messy roads to forgiveness. Take Beyoncé's aforementioned *Lemonade* — an artistic journey from betrayal to redemption. Or Adele's songs that sometimes hint at infidelity and the aftermath (hello, "Rolling in the Deep" rage and then later more conciliatory tones in "Water Under the Bridge"). We have entire reality TV series (like *VH1's Couples Therapy*) where celebrity couples air out their post-cheating issues on camera. It's raw and sometimes cringe, but also cathartic to see that even the rich and famous have to do the hard work if they want to stay together.

And what about those who don't forgive? Sometimes, The Fury (as in this chapter's title) takes over. Betrayed partners might enact a bit of dramatic vengeance to cope. We've all heard the tales (or seen the movies): the cheating husband comes home to find his clothes burned on the lawn. The cheating wife's precious car gets keyed or, in extreme cases, driven into a swimming pool. Our culture secretly cheers these acts of revenge – they make great country songs, after all. (Cue Carrie Underwood's "Before He Cheats," detailing how she took a Louisville slugger to her man's truck and carved her name into his leather seats. Zero forgiveness there – just a bat and some sweet, sweet retribution in 3/4 time.)

Then there are those who channel pain into personal growth. Shakira, for instance, recently went through a nasty breakup with soccer star Gerard Piqué, who allegedly cheated. Did she forgive? Not exactly – she wrote scathing hit songs about it (one lyric basically says "You traded a Ferrari (her) for a Twingo (the other woman)") and moved on with her life, *mic drop*. Sometimes "forget you" (in stronger language) is the message rather than forgive. And that's okay too – leaving can be the healthiest choice.

In the *aftermath*, there's also the broader impact on friends and family. Kids caught in the crossfire of a public affair have to process that one parent hurt the other. Some couples choose to be very open with their children (age-appropriately), others shield them from details. Public figures might issue statements asking for privacy for the family – often right after the scandal breaks. The irony is rich: a celebrity courts the limelight until it shows something unflattering, then suddenly, privacy please! Yet, you can't blame them for wanting to handle the aftermath away from prying eyes.

One surprising element in many affair aftermaths is hope. As dark as things get, humans have a remarkable capacity to hope and to heal. Therapists often say that couples who survive infidelity can emerge with a stronger, more honest relationship. It sounds paradoxical, but by tearing everything down, they were forced to rebuild from scratch, this time without the illusions. It's like a house renovation after a fire – painful and costly, but the new structure might be sturdier. There's a term, "post-traumatic growth," which can apply here; some individuals, and relationships, come out of the trauma of an affair with new insights, closer bonds, or a clearer sense of priorities. For example, a couple might finally address long-ignored issues: the affair spotlighted cracks that needed fixing (lack of intimacy, poor communication, etc.). If they manage to fix them, they sometimes report being happier *after* the storm than before it.

Of course, this isn't a Disney movie guarantee. For every couple that grows, there's one that simply can't recover the trust. They may try for a while – awkward dinners, checking each other's phones, sleeping in separate bedrooms – but eventually realize the love died on the vine of betrayal. And so they part ways, hopefully having learned something (like, say, *don't cheat on future partners* might be a good lesson). Some divorced exes even manage to become friends or at least civil co-parents, turning a new page entirely.

In the gallery of famous forgiveness (or lack thereof), one must mention Jay-Z and Beyoncé again, because their aftermath was practically a blueprint. They did the counseling, they made the art, and Jay-Z publicly acknowledged his wrongs in interviews (a rare thing for such a private couple). *"We did the hard work of going to therapy,"* he shared, implying that unpacking his childhood trauma helped him understand why he cheated – not to excuse it, but to ensure it never recurred. He said seeing the pain he caused Beyoncé was the hardest part, and that most men (or people in general) run from that, but he chose to stay. They even renewed their vows later, as seen in concert footage. That's some Hallmark-level healing right there. On the other hand, consider someone like Kevin Hart, the comedian who cheated on his pregnant wife and then very publicly atoned (including a whole Netflix documentary series about earning back her trust). His wife Eniko did take him back, but not before making him sweat and grovel, which he did. She said in an interview that *"choosing to forgive is the hardest thing I've ever had to do."* You can feel the residual hurt in that statement.

It's worth noting that cultural attitudes play a role in the aftermath too. In some cultures, there's pressure to forgive and save the marriage at all costs (for family honor, kids, religion, etc.). In others, there's an expectation that you kick the bum out immediately to preserve your self-respect. Public figures often face a PR calculus: will staying and forgiving make me look strong or like a doormat? Will leaving make me look empowered or vindictive? These considerations shouldn't matter, but in reality, they weigh on people, famous or not. Everyone and their aunt has an opinion when infidelity comes to light (*"I could never forgive that"* or *"You should at least try to work it out"*). Ultimately, only the people in the relationship know what's right for them.

As we wrap up this chapter, let's end on a note of cautious optimism. Yes, infidelity is gut-wrenching. It's called betrayal for a reason – it cuts deep. But the *fury* of the initial discovery doesn't have to be the final chapter. Some couples do find a path to a new normal. It might not be the fairy tale they originally envisioned (the shattered trust may never be *quite* as pristine as before), but it can be *enough* to keep writing their story together. They forgive (though they don't forget), and they move on – sometimes even cracking dark jokes about "that time you almost burned down our life." Other times, the healthiest choice is to close the book and start a new one with someone else, or solo. Forgiveness is optional; self-respect is not.

In the grand theatre of love and betrayal, the aftermath is the most private act – the quiet epilogue after the public drama. Whether it's reconciliation like Beyoncé and Jay-Z's highly poetic journey, or a parting of ways like so many others, there's always a chance for a new beginning. As one therapist quipped, "I see infidelity as either a tombstone or a turning point." In other words, it can mark the death of a relationship, or the rebirth of it in a new form.

For those who choose the turning point, it requires immense work, humility, and yes, love. For those who see the tombstone, it's a chance to mourn, then eventually heal and perhaps love again with someone new. Either way, life moves forward. People survive these storms – bruised but wiser.

So, dear reader, if you ever find yourself in an affair's wake (on either side of it), remember that while the *affair* brings the fire and fury, the *aftermath* is where the real story lies. It can be a story of forgiveness, or a story of a fierce new beginning alone – and often a bit of both. And if nothing else, it makes for one heck of a chapter in the book of life, one you'll recount with either a cringe or a chuckle (or both) years down the line. As they say, time heals all wounds... and wounds all heels.

Jaw-dropping truth of the aftermath: sometimes, against all odds, couples do emerge from the ashes stronger – case in point, Jay-Z has openly credited therapy for saving his marriage and helping him and Beyoncé find understanding after his cheating, rather than joining the 50% who divorce. And in other cases, moving on separately leads to personal triumphs – the betrayed partner may find new love or achieve goals they put on hold. There's no one-size-fits-all ending here. Just human beings muddling through, sometimes choosing love over pride, other times choosing self-worth over compromise. In the grand saga of "Cheaters, Lies, and Alibis," the final act is unwritten until we live it. And whether it ends in forgiveness or a fabulous solo journey, it's an ending *you* get to write – hopefully having learned a lesson or two from all the juicy tales we've explored (or at least having been entertained by them!).

Chapter 6
Royal Snafus and Historic Heartbreaks

Love has a way of turning even the most powerful royals into *absolute hot messes*. In this chapter, we'll take a witty whirlwind tour through four legendary romantic fiascos that rocked kingdoms and empires. From a king who literally created a new church to break up with his wife, to an emperor who sent love letters like a smitten teenager, history proves that when it comes to romance, even royals can royally screw up. Strap in for "Royal Snafus and Historic Heartbreaks", a satirical look at love gone wrong in high places.

Henry VIII and His Six Wives: Heir Today, Gone Tomorrow

Meet King Henry VIII of England, a man so desperate for a male heir that he left a trail of marital mayhem worthy of a reality TV show (working title: *"The Real Housewives of Tudor England"*). Henry is famous for having six wives – and an extremely short fuse when they didn't give him sons. In fact, British schoolchildren still recite a cheery little rhyme to remember the wives' fates: *"Divorced, Beheaded, Died; Divorced, Beheaded, Survived"*. Yes, Henry's quest for a male heir led him to divorce two wives and behead two others, sparking nothing less than a religious revolution. Talk about extra – this king didn't just change his Facebook status, he changed his country's entire faith!

Henry's first wife was Catherine of Aragon, a Spanish princess who unfortunately bore him only a daughter (the future Mary I) and no surviving sons. By his logic, this was an *unacceptable* situation – as if a girl heir just wouldn't do in a 16th-century boys' club. When the Pope refused to grant Henry an annulment, Henry essentially said, "Fine, I'll do it myself!" like a supervillain of matrimony. He broke from the Catholic Church and created the Church of England just so he could dump Catherine and marry a younger woman. That's right – he started his own church in 1533 mainly to *legally divorce*. It was the nuclear option of breakups: Henry literally reshaped England's religion for the sake of his love life. (Eat your heart out, reality TV divorce dramas – you've got nothing on the Reformation.)

The new bride was Anne Boleyn, a charismatic lady-in-waiting who had caught Henry's eye. Henry was obsessed; he showered Anne with gifts and titles, convinced she'd give him the coveted son. Spoiler: Anne gave birth to a daughter (the future Elizabeth I), and subsequent pregnancies ended in miscarriages. Henry, ever the reasonable chap, decided this must be *witchcraft or God's punishment* – clearly it couldn't be *his* fault. Anne's flirtatious and outspoken manner didn't help her case. In a move that still shocks (and darkly amuses) people today, Henry had Anne arrested on trumped-up charges of adultery and treason – alleging even an affair with her own brother – and promptly beheaded her in 1536. She became the first English queen to be publicly executed. Henry, showing the sensitivity of a man who changes wives like socks, married Wife #3 Jane Seymour just over a week later. (Nothing says "I'm over you" like remarrying before your decapitated ex is even cold.)

At last, luck smiled on Henry: Jane Seymour bore him a son, the future Edward VI. Henry was over the moon – his lifelong dream achieved. But in a cruel twist (or perhaps karma?), Jane died shortly after childbirth. Henry was genuinely heartbroken at Jane's death; rumor has it she was the only wife he truly mourned. Still, the king's heir hunger was temporarily sated – he had his male heir, so all was forgiven... until he got *restless* again.

Wife #4 was Anne of Cleves, a German princess picked via royal blind date. Famously, Henry agreed to marry her based on a flattering portrait (Tudor-era *catfishing*, anyone?). When Anne arrived, Henry took one look and was horrified – he declared she looked like a "Flanders mare," basically comparing her to a horse. Not exactly a gentleman. Their marriage went unconsummated (Henry blamed her appearance for being unable to perform his "husbandly duties") and both parties happily agreed to an annulment after six months. Anne of Cleves smartly accepted a generous settlement and outlived Henry, laughing all the way to the Tudor bank. She even became known as the "King's Beloved Sister" and got to keep her head (a pretty good outcome given the alternatives).

Henry's midlife crisis then led him to Catherine Howard, Wife #5 and a vivacious teenager five songs and a dance away from a TikTok career (had TikTok existed in 1540). Henry was nearly 50, obese, and plagued by a bad leg, but he was besotted with young Catherine, calling her his "rose without a thorn." The court gossiped that Catherine wasn't exactly an innocent maiden – she had a *past*. But Henry wouldn't hear it and married her anyway. Predictably, this ended badly. Catherine, bored with her gouty old husband, resumed an affair with a young courtier not long after the wedding. Big mistake: when Henry found out, he went full-on rage mode. Catherine Howard was executed for adultery and treason after just 17 months of marriage. Henry was said to be inconsolable and actually *wept* at her downfall – ironic, considering he ordered it.

By this point, our jolly monarch was ageing, ailing, and perhaps finally learning that chopping and changing (literally) wasn't bringing him happiness. Enter Catherine Parr, the sixth and last wife. Twice-widowed and intelligent, Catherine Parr was more of a nurse and companion to the ailing Henry than a romantic flame. She managed the impossible: she survived. Catherine Parr not only outlived Henry (no small feat) but even helped reconcile him with his daughters Mary and Elizabeth, providing a semblance of normal family life in his final years. She nearly got herself arrested once (for debating religion with the king – bold move, Cathy), but she skillfully talked her way out of it. When Henry died in 1547, Catherine Parr could claim the coveted title of "Survived" in that famous rhyme. After years of turmoil, Henry VIII left behind three heirs (Edward, Mary, Elizabeth) and a religiously transformed England – *and* he cemented his legacy as the poster child for royal romantic absurdity. I mean, creating a new Church just because the Pope wouldn't let you divorce? That's a flex of historic proportions. Henry's life shows that when royals follow their hearts, heads might literally roll.

Before we leave Tudor-land, let's just acknowledge the absurdity: Henry VIII's love life was basically a six-season series with twist endings no screenwriter would dare invent. From wife #2 onward, the pattern was clear – if you displeased the king, you either lost your crown, your head, or both. It's dark comedy at its finest. And yet, we can't look away. In a modern context, Henry's antics would dominate Twitter (imagine the memes!). Perhaps it's no surprise he's still a household name – part terrifying tyrant, part cautionary tale of how *not* to handle your marriages. Henry VIII wanted to be an all-powerful monarch and a prolific patriarch, but in chasing those male heirs he left behind a trail of royal snafus for the ages.

Mark Antony and Cleopatra: A Scandalous Love to Die For

If Henry VIII's story was a dark comedy, the saga of Mark Antony and Cleopatra is an epic tragedy with an extra dash of melodrama – *Romeo and Juliet* meets *House of Cards*. This famed Roman-Egyptian power couple turned the ancient world upside down with their political-romantic entanglement. Picture it: one of Rome's top generals, Mark Antony, falls head over sandals for Cleopatra VII, the alluring Queen of Egypt. Their affair was the talk of the Mediterranean – and not in a cute celebrity gossip way, but in a "Holy Jupiter, he's betraying Rome!" kind of way. Antony and Cleopatra's love was *so* all-consuming it practically toppled an empire, sparking scandal and war, and ending with not one but two dramatic suicides (featuring snakes, no less).

The pair met in 41 B.C., after Julius Caesar's assassination. Cleopatra had famously been Caesar's lover before (one does wonder if Rome had a *"Cleopatra Anonymous" support group for jealous Roman wives).

When Mark Antony summoned Cleopatra to answer some political charges, she didn't just show up like any old defendant – oh no. Cleopatra arrived in style, sailing up the Kydnos River on a golden barge dressed as the goddess Venus. She knew how to make an entrance. Antony – a man who enjoyed a good party – was *instantly* enchanted. The two spent the winter of 41–40 B.C. in Alexandria in what historians delicately describe as "debauchery" (basically an ancient Vegas bender). Imagine the headlines today: *"Top Roman General Skips Work, Parties with Egyptian Queen – Senate Furious!"* Indeed, while Antony was wining, dining, and canoodling with Cleopatra, back in Rome his political rivals were sharpening their knives.

To pacify Roman opinion (and Octavian, his fellow triumvir), Antony returned to Rome and even married Octavian's sister, Octavia in 40 B.C., in a bid to show he was still a team player. But political marriages have nothing on true passion – a few years later Antony ditched Octavia and raced back to Cleopatra's arms in the East. Cleopatra bore him *three* children (including twins) during their affair. The Roman public was scandalized: not only was Antony neglecting his proper Roman wife, he was acting like an Eastern king! In 34 B.C., the couple held a grand spectacle in Alexandria known as the "Donations of Alexandria," where Antony and Cleopatra sat on golden thrones and he doled out Roman territories to Cleopatra's children as if he were Santa at a very weird Christmas. To Romans, this was the ultimate betrayal – it looked like Antony was handing over the Roman Empire to a foreign seductress and her kids. Octavian (the future Emperor Augustus) pounced on this propaganda gift. He painted Cleopatra as a sneaky Eastern enchantress who had bewitched poor Antony and would ruin Rome if not stopped. It was basically an ancient smear campaign: Cleopatra was the *Yoko Ono* breaking up the Roman Beatles.

By 32 B.C., things went from soap opera to full-on war. Octavian declared war on Cleopatra (pointedly, *not* on Antony – Romans still couldn't fathom that their homegrown hero was willingly in cahoots with her). The decisive clash came at the Battle of Actium in 31 B.C., a naval showdown in Greek waters. Legend says Cleopatra was personally there with her ships. When the battle turned against them, Cleopatra's fleet suddenly fled the scene, and Antony – love-struck fool that he was – broke off the fight and followed her with his own ships. The remaining Antony forces, now leaderless, surrendered. It was a disastrous defeat – one could say Antony "left his empire hanging" because he couldn't resist chasing his queen. (Modern parallel: imagine a top general abandoning a critical mission because he saw a text from his ex – that's the level of head-smack foolishness here.)

After Actium, Antony and Cleopatra holed up in Egypt as Octavian closed in. Fast forward to 30 B.C. in Alexandria: Octavian's armies are at the city gates, Antony's troops have melted away, and our lovers are cornered. Here's where it reaches Shakespearean heights of drama (indeed Shakespeare *did* immortalize it). Amid the chaos, Cleopatra hatched a plan to test Antony's love (because apparently everything else wasn't proof enough). Various ancient sources claim she sent word that she had died – perhaps hoping to spur Antony to action or as a desperate ploy. It worked *too* well. **On hearing (falsely) that Cleopatra was dead,

Mark Antony was devastated and stabbed himself with his sword. Talk about an extreme reaction – this was the real-life prototype for every tragic romantic hero. But plot twist: Antony didn't die immediately from the wound, and soon he learned Cleopatra was actually alive. In a scene that begs for a Hollywood close-up, the dying Antony was brought to Cleopatra's hiding place (some say she refused to come out, so he was hauled to her) and he died in Cleopatra's arms – allegedly urging her to make peace with Octavian in his final breaths. It's heart-wrenching, yes, but also a bit *facepalm*. If only they had cell phones to clarify the miscommunication! It's the classic tragic timing: he thought she was gone, so he offed himself; she finds him dying and now *she's* truly alone against Rome.

Cleopatra, now a lone queen without her Roman lover, faced a grim future. Octavian wanted to parade her in chains in his triumph back in Rome – a fate she found worse than death. Cleopatra was ever the dramatic artiste, and she resolved to exit the stage on her own terms. In August 30 B.C., after negotiating with Octavian and realizing he was not about to let her remain queen, Cleopatra took her own life. And of course, she did it in the most theatrical way possible: according to tradition, she provoked a venomous asp (snake) to bite her. Yes, a snakebite suicide – the queen of extra till the end. The asp's venom killed her swiftly (along with two of her faithful handmaidens who also chose death). Ancient accounts note that the asp was likely smuggled to her in a basket of figs, and Cleopatra adorned herself in her royal regalia before applying the serpent. The symbolism was rich: the asp's bite was seen as a mark of divine royalty and a means for her to join her lover in death on her own terms. When Octavian finally laid hands on Cleopatra, it was as a corpse. He was reportedly furious – she had robbed him of a prize for his triumph.

Thus ended the tale of Antony and Cleopatra: two star-crossed lovers who brought each other to ruin in a blaze of passion and poison. Their double-suicide became the stuff of legend, inspiring countless paintings, plays, and movies (who can forget Liz Taylor and Richard Burton smoldering at each other?). It's easy to draw modern parallels: a powerful man risking career and country for the love of a beautiful, controversial woman – we see echoes of it in celebrity scandals and political downfalls today. The difference is, instead of reputations dying, in this case actual people did. Antony's name in Rome became synonymous with folly and betrayal, while Cleopatra got cast (unfairly) as a sinister temptress in Roman histories. But one can't deny the tragic romance at the heart of it. They could have won the world, but they chose each other – and lost everything. High drama? Check. Irony? Plenty (they literally died due to a *miscommunication* and some venomous pets). Modern take? Perhaps: love can make you do crazy things, but giving your enemies free snake bites might be taking it a bit far.

In a satirical light, you might say Antony and Cleopatra were the ultimate power couple gone wrong. If there had been tabloids in 30 B.C., the papyrus scrolls would scream: *"General Throws Away Empire for Love!"*, *"Queen and Roman in Death Pact – Snakes Involved!"*. It has all the elements of a bingeable series – passion, betrayal, war, and a twist ending. Their story endures as a cautionary tale: mix politics and romance at your peril, and maybe avoid relationships where the pet snake is plan B. The timeless chaos of their royal romance shows that sometimes love not only conquers all – it *destroys* all, too.

Napoleon and Josephine: Passion, Power, and Strategic Heartbreak

Jumping forward in time and tone, we arrive at the love life of Napoleon Bonaparte and Joséphine de Beauharnais – a tale that has all the trappings of a modern celebrity romance, except with imperial titles and armies at stake. If Antony and Cleopatra were a tragedy, Napoleon and Josephine are a romantic dramedy: passionate love letters, steamy affairs, over-the-top gestures, and a heartbreak so strategic it could only happen in politics. Think of them as the ultimate power couple of the 19th century, with a relationship as turbulent as a Napoleonic battlefield.

Napoleon Bonaparte, the ambitious Corsican turned French general, met Joséphine (born Marie-Josèphe-Rose, a glamorous Creole widow a few years his senior) in the mid-1790s. She was an it-girl of Parisian society – stylish, sophisticated, and a survivor of the guillotine terror (her first husband had literally lost his head in the Revolution). Napoleon fell *hard* for her. This man was conquering Europe but could not conquer his own heart. His letters to Joséphine are the stuff of legend – ardent, flowery, and frankly a little obsessive, as if written by a love-struck teenager rather than a general. "Every moment separates me further from you, my beloved... I have less energy to exist so far from you," he gushed from campaign, calling her the constant object of his thoughts. In one infamous note, he even instructed her not to bathe until he arrived home

– he *really* wanted her "natural scent." (Talk about TMI.) Another letter promised to cover her in "a million hot kisses, burning like the equator". In today's terms, Napoleon's texts would be screenshotted and shared in group chats for their sheer thirstiness. Joséphine, for her part, was flattered but not initially as infatuated; she allegedly teased that Napoleon was short and called him *"a little pussycat in boots"* (ouch). Nonetheless, she saw his rising star and married him in 1796. He was 26, she 32, and they became the *It Couple* of post-Revolutionary France.

For a while, it was bliss – or at least *blistering* passion. They spent only two days together as newlyweds before Napoleon had to leave to command the army in Italy. Away at war, he bombarded Joséphine with those love letters. Meanwhile, back in Paris, lonely Joséphine started an affair with a dashing cavalry officer, Hippolyte Charles. Yes, both partners in this iconic romance were adulterous – frequently and flagrantly. When Napoleon got wind of Joséphine's fling in 1798, he flew into a jealous rage. The conqueror of Italy was reduced to a hurt, angry husband. He even wrote to his brother complaining he might divorce her. Joséphine managed to smooth things over temporarily by playing the loving, apologetic wife (and Napoleon's deep love for her let him forgive... for the moment). But she didn't actually stop the affair right away, and soon enough Napoleon himself took a mistress during his Egyptian campaign (the relationship tit-for-tat was in full swing). By the time Napoleon returned to France in 1799, their marriage was a powder keg of passion and resentment. In one legendary episode, he came home unannounced from Egypt and caught Joséphine *literally* with her lover – she locked herself in her bedroom, and Napoleon, after stomping around furious, eventually cooled off. There was screaming, tears, door-slamming – reality TV producers could only dream of such drama.

Despite "affairs on both sides," a deep attachment grew – and endured. They genuinely loved each other in their own fiery way, and both were invested in the partnership. When Napoleon became Emperor of the French in 1804, he *crowned Joséphine as Empress* in a lavish ceremony at Notre-Dame Cathedral (famously, he took the crown from the Pope's hands and placed it on both his and her heads himself – talk about a power move). It was the pinnacle of their joint rise: from penniless widow and upstart general to Emperor and Empress in just a decade. At the coronation, in Jacques-Louis David's grand painting, Joséphine kneels before Napoleon looking every inch the devoted wife. But behind the scenes, the marriage was still rocky. Mere weeks before that ceremony, Joséphine had caught Napoleon in an affair with one of her ladies-in-waiting – cue another round of screaming matches. They patched it up enough for the public eye; appearances mattered now more than ever.

Ultimately, the issue that doomed their marriage wasn't infidelity – it was infertility (or at least the lack of a male heir). Napoleon desperately wanted a son to inherit his new empire. Joséphine had children from her first marriage but, by her 40s, she hadn't given Napoleon any offspring and it appeared she never would. In 1806, one of Napoleon's mistresses bore him a healthy son, proving the problem wasn't with his *Little Corporal* (if you catch our drift) but with Joséphine's age. Then Napoleon's beloved nephew (whom he'd considered heir) died in 1807, leaving him heirless. Ever the strategist, Napoleon began to see marriage as a duty to dynasty. With a heavy heart (and prodded by advisors), he made a drastic decision: he divorced Joséphine in 1809 so he could remarry and father a legitimate heir. But trust Napoleon to put a dramatic, bittersweet spin on it – this was no ordinary divorce; it was more like a state funeral for their love. At the official divorce ceremony, Napoleon and Joséphine both wept and read out statements of devotion to each other. In his speech, Napoleon praised Joséphine's sweetness and sacrifices, declaring "Far from ever finding cause for complaint, I can to the contrary only congratulate myself on the devotion and tenderness of my beloved wife". Joséphine, through tears, affirmed that she still loved him. Imagine a modern divorce where the couple is basically saying "I love you" as they sign the papers – it's almost absurdly sentimental. They ended their marriage *professing* mutual love, each essentially saying "it's not you, it's duty." It was the most amicably heart-breaking split imaginable – a "strategic heartbreak" indeed.

Napoleon didn't waste time securing that heir. He promptly married Marie-Louise, an Austrian princess (18 years old – prime childbearing age, because emperors are nothing if not pragmatic). Sure enough, she produced a son in 1811, duly named Napoleon II. Joséphine, now ex-Empress, was given titles and a comfortable retirement at her estate, Malmaison. Remarkably, Napoleon and Joséphine stayed in contact and on good terms after the divorce. He would occasionally send her letters, and she reportedly still called him "Bonaparte" affectionately. Joséphine even hosted Marie-Louise at Malmaison once (that must have been an awkward tea party – the ex-wife giving pointers to the new wife!).

Joséphine famously told someone, "I am not the wife of Napoleon, but I am still *Josephine*," savoring her unique place in his life.

When Joséphine died in 1814 (while Napoleon was in exile on Elba), he was distraught. And here's the kicker: Napoleon's last words on his deathbed in 1821 were reportedly "France, the Army, Joséphine". In his final moments, his grand empire in ruins, his thoughts returned to the woman who had owned his heart. It doesn't get more poetic (or cinematic) than that. Their love, with all its storms and scandals, endured in some form to the end. Even though he had married another, even though she was long gone, Napoleon's soul still whispered Joséphine's name. One could joke that even *death* couldn't break their emotional bond – the ultimate late-night drunk text, if you will, just without a phone.

The tale of Napoleon and Joséphine is the prototype of every "power couple" drama we see today: intense love, public image versus private reality, career pressures, and the tough choice between personal happiness and professional duty. It's almost modern in its relatability. Swap the letters for WhatsApp messages and the coronation for a red-carpet event, and you have a celebrity tabloid saga. They were the Kanye and Kim of their day (with fewer Instagram posts, more crowns). We have to give a cheeky nod to Joséphine as well – she navigated being Napoleon's wife with savvy, knew when to play the devoted partner and when to plead for mercy (like when divorce was first on the table). And Napoleon, conqueror of Europe, was utterly conquered by love. He won battles with brilliant strategy but lost himself in letters telling his wife how much he missed her scent. It's almost endearing to see the human side of the man often depicted as a stern military genius.

In satirical hindsight, one might imagine a counselor telling them: "Perhaps open marriage would suit you two?" They certainly acted on an open-ish arrangement at times. Or envision a reality TV confessional: Napoleon: *"I'm doing this for France – I need a son. But I still love Jo, always will."* Joséphine (sobbing): *"He was the love of my life, but I understand why he must leave."* The camera zooms out as she waves goodbye in front of an ornate palace, cue bittersweet music. Despite everything – the infidelities, the political calculations – their romance retains an almost sentimental glow. Time has been kinder to their love story than to many others, painting it as a grand, doomed romance. Perhaps because in the end, both Napoleon and Joséphine truly cared for each other, even when duty forced them apart. As Napoleon himself said later in life, "I truly loved my Joséphine, but I thought it my duty to marry a second time; I have not been happy since." Oof, that's a dagger right there.

Thus, Napoleon and Joséphine's chapter in our compendium of *royal snafus* illustrates the timeless chaos of love versus duty. They show us that even an emperor couldn't have it all: the empire *and* the love of his life intact. Something had to give. In their case, love was sacrificed on the altar of ambition – yet the embers of that love never died. It's romantic, it's absurd, it's touching, and it's a little infuriating (just have the baby with a surrogate, one wants to yell from the future!). And it's a reminder that the grandest figures in history were still, at the end of the day, people with hearts – hearts that could ache, yearn, and break just like anyone else's.

King Edward VIII and Wallis Simpson: The King Who Said "Nah" to the Crown

Our final stop is a royal scandal with a slightly more modern flavor – one that rocked the British monarchy in the 20th century and remains a benchmark for love-vs-duty dilemmas. It's the story of King Edward VIII and Wallis Simpson, a saga often summarized as *"the king who gave up his throne for love."* Snarky admiration is warranted here: you've got to be either hopelessly romantic or certifiably nuts (or a bit of both) to do what Edward did. This episode has all the makings of a juicy Netflix miniseries – oh wait, it's already depicted in *The Crown*. In December 1936, Edward VIII shocked the world by abdicating – literally quitting the top job of King-Emperor – because he refused to give up the woman he loved, Wallis Warfield Simpson, an American socialite who had not one but two ex-husbands living. That's right: the Supreme Governor of the Church of England wanted to marry a twice-divorced American, and the establishment just couldn't handle it.

To set the scene: Edward VIII became king in January 1936 upon the death of his father, George V. He was handsome, charismatic, and something of a playboy – the British public initially adored him. But behind the scenes, a constitutional crisis was brewing. Edward was deeply in love with Wallis Simpson, who was in the midst of divorcing her second husband. For the hidebound British government and the royal family, Wallis was beyond the pale: as a divorced (and soon-to-be twice-divorced) woman, and an American to boot, she would be an "unacceptable" queen consort. In that era, the Church of England (headed by the monarch) forbade remarriage of divorced people if their ex-spouses were still alive. The tabloids hadn't yet splashed the story, but the upper echelons knew Edward was serious about Wallis. Prime Minister Stanley Baldwin and others told the king flat-out: you cannot marry her and keep the throne. It was the ultimate ultimatum – love or duty.

For a while, the King tried to find a workaround. Could Wallis just be a morganatic wife (i.e. not queen, just wife)? The answer from the establishment: nope. Advisors basically said, "You'll cause the monarchy to collapse if you do this." (Imagine the group chat: *Church: "This marriage is a sin."* Government: "This will bring down the Empire."* Edward: "But I love her 😢."* Not going well.) The British public was mostly kept in the dark at first – but rumors swirled, and by December 1936 the scandal exploded in the press. Under unimaginable pressure and refusing to live without Wallis, Edward chose the nuclear option: he abdicated. On December 11, 1936, after less than a year on the throne, Edward VIII gave a radio broadcast to the nation, announcing he was leaving the crown for the woman he loved. In his famous words, *"I have found it impossible to carry the heavy burden of responsibility... without the help and support of the woman I love."* Those last four words – "the woman I love" – reverberated around the world. Some listeners swooned at the romance; others gasped at the irresponsibility. A king throwing away a thousand-year crown for love? It was unprecedented.

Let's be clear: this was the biggest royal romantic fiasco of the modern age. No British monarch had ever voluntarily stepped down because of a personal relationship. The fallout was immense. Edward's younger brother Albert ("Bertie" to the family) became King George VI (yes, the one with the stutter from *The King's Speech*), and he had to clean up the mess. The royal family was scandalized and not a little incensed at Edward. Ordinary Brits had mixed feelings – many were upset that he'd abandoned duty, others secretly admired the fairy-tale notion of giving up a kingdom for love. It was, in a sense, the ultimate love vs. duty showdown, played out on the world stage.

Wallis Simpson, for her part, was painted by sections of the British press as a conniving adventuress, a social climber who ensnared the king. (Sound familiar? Similar tropes get thrown at modern royal spouses in some tabloids – history echoes.) But to be fair, Edward was a grown man and a king – he made his own choices. He essentially said, *"To heck with being king if I can't have Wallis."* And off he went. After the abdication, Edward was given the title Duke of Windsor and whisked into exile. In 1937, he married Wallis in a small ceremony in France – notably, none of his family attended. The British establishment effectively ostracized the couple for years. It's both romantic and pathetic: romantic that he sacrificed everything for love; pathetic (to some) that he didn't sacrifice the love for everything.

Snarky commentary abounds. Some historians note that Edward wasn't terribly suited to be king anyway – he hated paperwork and protocol, and was perhaps relieved to ditch the job. (One might quip that he used the love story as a very convenient exit strategy from employment.) Also, uncomfortable fact: Edward and Wallis had a dubious fondness for Hitler's Germany. They even met Hitler in 1937, happily photographed smiling with him. This has led wags to comment that by abdicating, Edward inadvertently did the UK a favor – they avoided a potential Nazi-sympathizing monarch. History's irony: the "love conquers all" narrative overshadowed the potential that Edward VIII was a pretty poor excuse for a king anyway. As one snide commentator put it, "He achieved more by abdication than he ever did as king" – ouch.

From a cheeky perspective, imagine this saga in today's context: A reigning British king livestreams on Instagram, "Hey guys, so I'm quitting the family firm because y'know, my girlfriend's not welcome and love wins." The internet would break. In 1936, the medium was radio and newsreels, but the effect was similar – global shock and frenzy. The appeal of the Edward-Wallis story is undeniable: it's got that fairy-tale twist. Usually the prince *gets* the girl and the crown; here the prince got the girl by *dropping* the crown. It's upside-down and kind of fabulous in its scandalous way. Countless books, films, and shows have been made about them, and Wallis's line "You have no idea how hard it is to live out a great romance" captures the self-aware drama of their lives.

Let's sprinkle some modern analogies. Edward and Wallis were, in a sense, the OG "royal exit", long before Harry and Meghan's departure made headlines (though the circumstances differ greatly). Edward traded the literal throne for an unofficial life. It's as if a modern CEO resigned via tweet saying, "Can't do it without my boo, so I quit." The dedication is sweet, but the board of directors (or in this case, the British government) was not amused. The British Empire in 1936 was still vast, and its figurehead just checked out because of matters of the heart. One parliamentarian lamented, *"Which is the greater gesture? To renounce the woman you love for the sake of your people, or renounce your people for the sake of the woman you love?"* Edward chose the latter, and that was a very un-British thing for a monarch to do at the time. Duty was supposed to come first, stiff upper lip and all that. Edward chucked that script and followed his heart to France.

The aftermath: Edward and Wallis became the Duke and Duchess of Windsor and lived mostly abroad, floating around Europe and occasionally popping in to annoy the royal family with ill-advised comments. They had no children. They threw lavish parties, rubbed shoulders with the elite (and dictators), and were essentially celebrities living off pensions and wealthy friends. Some admired them as a couple who genuinely stuck together against the odds – they stayed married until Edward's death in 1972. Others saw their life as hollow: exiled, trivial, and a bit sad, with Wallis forever the woman blamed for a king's fall. It's all in how you spin it – tragedy or triumph?

In a satirical retelling, one might picture Wallis quipping, "I *really* didn't mean for him to lose his job!" and Edward saying, "Well, it seemed like a good idea at the time." The whole scenario is ripe for cheeky commentary. For example, British wits later joked that the monarchy survived because it traded *Edward for George* – a playboy for a dutiful family man (George VI). The lovebirds in exile became something of a sideshow. When asked about the abdication years later, Wallis reportedly said, *"You have no idea how hard it is to be a royal without a kingdom – the tiara doesn't come with spending money."* (Okay, we made that quote up – but it fits their predicament.)

Ultimately, King Edward VIII and Wallis Simpson's romance stands as a testament to the crazy things people (even kings) will do for love. It's equal parts inspiring and baffling. Inspiring in that Edward didn't care about literally being Emperor of India if he couldn't have his chosen partner – that's one for the romance history books. Baffling in that he upended an ancient institution and probably didn't fully grasp the consequences (his brother had to lead a nation through World War II largely unprepared because *surprise*, he was king now). The satirical angle writes itself: Did Edward read too many romance novels? Was Wallis's allure truly worth an empire? (She was chic, yes, but can any relationship beat being *King of England?* Edward's answer: Yes, hers can.) The British establishment's reaction was summed up by a government minister: *"That boy threw away the throne for a woman – imagine!"* (spoken with utter horror). To which a modern romantic might reply: *"Aw, he really loved her, get over it."*

In the grand tapestry of royal romances, Edward and Wallis are like the quirky chapter where the prince *doesn't* follow the script. Instead of *"happily ever after on the throne,"* it's *"happily ever after in exile."* And frankly, they seemed content enough with that bargain. Edward's famous broadcast not only shook the monarchy, it added a new phrase to the lexicon of love. "The Woman I Love" became shorthand for choosing love over all else. We give it a snarky salute – it was a scandal, a fiasco, but undeniably a heck of a love story.

Conclusion: Across these tales – from Henry VIII's marital chopping block, to Antony and Cleopatra's poisonous climax, to Napoleon and Josephine's bittersweet strategy, and Edward VIII's abdication for love – a common thread emerges: the timeless chaos of royal romance. Powerful people making *spectacularly* personal decisions, often at odds with their duty or commonsense, is a recipe for historic heartache and occasional farce. It seems no matter the century or the continent, when love and power collide, drama ensues. These couples lived in different eras under different circumstances, yet their stories all provoke that mix of laughter, awe, and head-shaking disbelief that only true stories can. They remind us that kings and queens, emperors and generals – for all their wealth and power – are still driven by the most basic of human impulses: love, lust, longing, ego, fear. In other words, they're just as prone to snafus and heartbreaks as the rest of us, albeit on a more spectacular stage.

So, whether it's Henry composing a new religion to ditch a wife, or Cleopatra brandishing a snake to join her lover in the afterlife, or Napoleon penning XOXO letters from the battlefield, or Edward signing away a kingdom with a quiver in his voice – we can chuckle and cringe at the extremes they went to. History's lovers often *are* fools, but they are *our* fools, endearingly and enduringly so. And frankly, their misadventures make for great stories – ones that continue to captivate us, teach us, and entertain us with the grand theater of what happens when royal hearts overrule royal heads. Each fiasco is a firm reminder: crowns may be heavy, but the human heart can be heavier, and woe betide the realm when the latter wins out. In the contest of love vs. duty, these four couples serve up four very different outcomes – comedic, tragic, bittersweet, and scandalous – yet each in their own way demonstrates that age-old truth: the course of true love never did run smooth, especially not when thrones are involved. And boy, isn't that good news for us lovers of a juicy story?

Chapter 7

Love in the Limelight – Celebrity Lessons in Lunacy

Welcome to the circus of celebrity romance, where love is a spectacle and heartbreak sells magazines. If normal relationships can be a little crazy, then famous ones are downright certifiable. In this chapter, we're diving into the wildest love lessons that Hollywood and pop culture have to offer. Buckle up: it's going to be a bumpy, hilarious ride through four cautionary tales of passion and folly under the spotlight.

Liz and Dick: A Hollywood Love Too Big for One Marriage

Elizabeth Taylor and Richard Burton—known to the world simply as "Liz and Dick"—gave Hollywood one of its most iconic love sagas. Their romance was so colossal it couldn't be contained in one marriage; they actually divorced and remarried just to ride the whole rollercoaster. It all started on the set of *Cleopatra*, where a steamy on-screen kiss spilled over into an off-screen affair that ignited an international scandal. (Imagine "breaking the internet," 1960s-style – the Pope even publicly condemned them. You know your love life is wild when it earns a papal scolding.)

From there, Liz and Dick delivered a masterclass in high-drama passion. Their fights were as legendary as their makeups. They bickered in public and private with equal gusto—Elizabeth once quipped their fights were "delightful screaming matches," likening Richard's temper to a small atom bomb. Burton admitted they sometimes staged fights "for the benefit of the mob," since the public expected nothing less from such a glamorous duo. Think of it as performance art meets couples therapy, with champagne and the occasional flying vase as props.

And oh, did they love to perform. Paparazzi stalked them relentlessly—they practically invented the modern paparazzi frenzy. They even discovered fans renting the hotel room below theirs just to eavesdrop on arguments; obligingly, Liz joked, she and Richard gave those snoops an earful. If people treated their relationship like theater, they figured they might as well put on a show. (When you get aroused playing Scrabble with your spouse—Liz's own example of "that's love, baby"—you know the passion is off the charts.)

When they weren't fighting (or, ahem, making up), Liz and Dick were busy proving their love with conspicuous extravagance. They didn't settle for flowers and date nights; they did yachts on the Mediterranean, bought mansions around the globe, and even impulse-bought a private jet one afternoon, as casually as grabbing gum at checkout. That's love, Old Hollywood style: go big or go get another marriage.

Yet for all the glamour, the messy truth at the heart of Liz and Dick's saga was that love isn't a smooth ride for anyone, not even superstars. They adored each other madly—couldn't live without each other—but often could barely live *with* each other either. One minute they were exchanging diamond gifts, the next exchanging insults. There were epic binges and jealous blowups; at one point Elizabeth chased a young starlet out of Richard's suite brandishing a vodka bottle as a weapon. (Nothing says "I love you" like threatening to clobber a potential rival.) Richard wasn't innocent either—his wandering eye fueled plenty of marital explosions worthy of a soap opera.

After a decade of this glamorous chaos, they finally blew apart in the mid-70s under the weight of too many fights (and far too much whiskey). But even divorce couldn't keep them apart. In true Hollywood fashion, they remarried for a short-lived sequel that lasted less than a year before imploding again. "I don't want to be that much in love ever again," Liz confided after the dust settled, exhausted from the rollercoaster. Sometimes even epic love has an expiration date—in their case, two.

Remarkably, Liz and Dick never completely quit each other. Even post-divorce, they stayed in contact, bound by a connection neither could fully shake. Burton wrote Taylor passionate letters for years (reportedly one just days before his death, longing to "come home"). They simply couldn't let go. If there's one lesson in lunacy from Liz and Dick, it's that passionate love can be as magnificent as it is messy. Love isn't always a fairy tale; sometimes it's a booze-soaked, diamond-studded carnival ride that leaves even icons dizzy. And while most of us won't be hurling vodka bottles or buying jets to prove our love, we can all relate to the way it makes even the sanest people a little crazy. At least our worst romantic blowups aren't captured by paparazzi – Liz and Dick never had that luxury.

Reality TV Romance – When Producers Play Cupid

Once upon a time, you had to *be* famous to have your love life turn into public entertainment. Now, thanks to reality TV, any bold soul can volunteer to find love on national television. Shows like *The Bachelor* and *Love Island* have made dating a spectator sport, complete with dramatic rose ceremonies and viewers munching popcorn through your every kiss and crisis. The premise sounds almost wholesome—a bunch of singles looking for love in a fabulous location. The reality? It's a carefully engineered circus of romance and humiliation, a shameless mix of beauty pageant, game show, and soap opera where the champagne is free and the tears are very real.

The formula is as simple as it is insane. Take a couple dozen attractive, emotionally excitable people and sequester them in a mansion or island villa. Take away their phones, add copious alcohol and a hot tub (or three), and let the drama marinate. One minute someone's making out under the stars; the next they're sobbing on a balcony because their new flame is making out under the stars with someone else. It's a roller coaster of feelings, like a high school prom that never ends—if prom had a camera crew and an endless supply of roses.

The producers, of course, are the puppet masters. If a couple seems *too* happy, they'll toss in a seductive "bombshell" newcomer to turn heads and spark jealousy. Things getting dull? Cue a twist: a stolen kiss during a group date, an ex showing up unexpectedly, or a bizarre challenge (synchronized skydiving, anyone?) designed to create maximum awkwardness. Contestants often say they're on an emotional roller coaster; they're not wrong—except the producers built the track and are gleefully controlling the speed.

Then come the familiar characters and catchphrases. There's always the earnest soul babbling about their "journey" and being there "for the right reasons" (drink every time you hear that). There's the designated villain declaring "I'm not here to make friends!" right on cue. Sooner or later, we get the mascara-streaked meltdown—because apparently dating *"the love of your life"* is really hard when you're sharing them with a dozen rivals in a hot tub. And of course, the finale features an implausibly shiny engagement ring and two semi-strangers professing love while a camera crane dramatically swoops overhead. It's supposed to be a fairy tale, but it often feels more like a farce with very good lighting.

What's funny is that for all the fakery, the feelings are often genuine. Sure, the scenario is absurd, but jealousy is jealousy whether it's on a reality show or at your office happy hour. Who hasn't felt insecure when a crush gives attention elsewhere? These shows just amplify everything. The Bachelor forgetting someone's name on a group date? That's every awkward first date ever (just edited to a soundtrack). The Love Island fight over a flirty glance? We've all had dumb squabbles sparked by misunderstandings—though usually without six cameras filming and an audience tweeting about it.

If there's a lesson here, it's that love makes people a little crazy even without producers pulling strings—add them in, and all bets are off. And yet we keep watching, equal parts romantic and voyeur. We secretly hope the final couple lives happily ever after, even as we relish the trainwreck moments along the way. At the very least, it's comforting: no matter how bumpy our own dating lives get, at least we're not doing it with a mic on and millions judging our every move. The next time you endure an awkward Tinder date, just remember: you could be in a mansion, in formal wear, ugly-crying on national TV because someone you met last week isn't "here for the right reasons."

Of course, even without a camera crew or a producer handing out date cards, celebrities manage to create plenty of romantic chaos. For that, let's look at the original masters of high-budget heartbreak…

Rockstars and Heartbreakers

You don't need a television producer to find an outrageous love story. Rockstars, movie idols, and famous folks of all stripes have managed fine on their own. In fact, some of pop culture's messiest romances were completely unscripted – you might even say improvised disasters. We've all heard the tales: the iconic rocker swapping supermodels like guitar picks, leaving a trail of scorned exes; the glamorous co-stars who fell madly in love on set, only to see their union go up in flames under paparazzi pressure; the pop princess who married a guy in Vegas on a whim and annulled it 55 hours later; the actor who slid into a model's DMs for a fling that fizzled faster than a TikTok trend. The names change, but the patterns stay the same.

One hallmark of these high-wattage affairs is the intensity. When celebs fall in love, they fall hard and fast, often with grand gestures normal people would (wisely) avoid. Matching tattoos on the second date? Sure, why not. A spontaneous getaway to Paris after a week together? Sounds like a music video, so they do it. It's great for the highlight reel, but reality is less forgiving: tattoos last longer than many Hollywood hookups, and impulsive trips don't mix well with busy schedules and bigger egos.

And the breakups—oh, the breakups. Where you or I might have a difficult "we need to talk" conversation, stars have full-blown public sagas. They break up via splashy headlines, Insta-live confessionals, or messy Twitter feuds. We've seen the joint PR statement asking for "privacy during this time" (as if the whole world wasn't just privy to their Instagram war). Some splits devolve into legal battles and even diss tracks. One famous rocker reportedly informed his wife it was over via fax machine (apparently he missed the memo that Hallmark doesn't make a "I'm divorcing you" card). Another Hollywood bad boy left an ex a voicemail tantrum so outrageous that it leaked online, turning their private meltdown into a public scandal. When celebrities part ways, it's rarely simple or dignified; it's a high-budget circus and we're all invited to grab popcorn.

The irony is that money and fame don't make anyone better at relationships. In fact, they can make it harder. Imagine being told "yes" by everyone around you, and then your partner says "no" — some stars just don't know how to handle it. Or being adored by millions of fans, then coming home to someone who isn't impressed by your celebrity one bit. Add in crazy work schedules, constant travel, and endless temptation, and it's a wonder any famous couple stays together. Love doesn't care how famous you are; if you neglect it or take it for granted, it will fall apart all the same.

So what can we regular folks take from these rockstar romances gone wrong? First, be glad your worst breakup wasn't broadcast to the world. However bad it was, at least millions of strangers weren't weighing in on Twitter. Second, maybe think twice before tattooing someone's name on your body (seriously, that rarely ends well). And finally, find solace in the fact that even people who seem to "have it all" can be total disasters in love. The rich and famous screw up relationships just like the rest of us — if anything, they do it in grander fashion. It's reassuring, in a way: no matter how high we climb, we're all a little foolish when our heart's on the line.

Speaking of all of us… in the age of social media, the spotlight isn't just for the rich and famous anymore. Now everyone with a phone can put their love on center stage — for better or worse…

Love in the Age of Instagram

Social media has blurred the line between celebrity and everyone else. Welcome to love in the age of Instagram, where every couple – famous or not – can broadcast a highlight reel of their romance. For celebrities, it's both a blessing and a curse. On one hand, they can curate the narrative: post a cuddly selfie to squash breakup rumors, or share a carefully worded notes-app announcement when a split is official. On the other hand, fans have become digital sleuths. Did he delete all her photos? Did she stop wearing her engagement ring? Instantly the gossip mill churns: *OMG, did they break up?* In this era, the unfollow button is as telling as a press release.

There's also the ritual of going "Instagram official." It's not real (so they say) until it's on the grid. Celeb couples often debut with a perfectly posed photo timed for maximum buzz. Regular people play along too: first a soft-launch (maybe a casual story featuring an unidentified hand or second coffee cup), then the full couple selfie on the feed. Cue the chorus of heart-eye emojis from friends and the passive-aggressive "you two look so happy" from that one ex. Modern love isn't just lived; it's performed for an audience.

And when things go wrong? There's a script for that, too. First comes the Instagram purge: one day your profile is full of cute couple pics, the next it's like your ex never existed. (Everyone notices the disappearance of those photos immediately, trust me.) Then the passive-aggressive posts start. One might share a pointed quote about "betrayal and new beginnings," while the other posts a selfie captioned "Living my best life 😌 ." Translation: they're subtweeting each other in plain view. Finally, the grand finale – the dreaded joint statement, often presented as a screenshot of a typed note. "We have decided to part ways but remain the closest of friends. We will always love each other. We kindly ask for privacy," etc., etc. Both parties post it at the same time like a coordinated dance. Within minutes, fans lament "love is dead 🪦 ," gossip sites dissect every line, and the breakup becomes a full-on public spectacle. Breaking up has never been so choreographed.

The kicker is, it's not only celebs doing this dance. Plenty of non-famous folks mimic it too. We all know a couple who overshares their #love online – until suddenly they don't. The lovey-dovey posts dry up, and cryptic Taylor Swift lyrics start popping up on their Stories. Social media encourages us to curate our relationships just like celebrities do, glossing over the cracks and highlighting the sparkly bits. After all, who wants to post "we argued for three hours last night" when you can post "look at the gorgeous bouquet bae surprised me with!" We're all crafting a narrative.

But behind every Instagram filter are real people with real problems. No amount of Valencia or Clarendon can paper over serious issues or the everyday work a relationship requires. Even the most #blessed couples on your feed have bad days, petty fights, and unflattering angles. They just don't share those. Every relationship has a blooper reel that stays off-camera.

So whether it's A-listers subtweeting exes or your co-worker flooding Facebook with sappy anniversary tributes, remember to take it all with a grain of salt. Love in the limelight – even if it's just the glow of your phone screen – is part reality, part fantasy. Everyone's starring in their own little romantic drama online, but nobody's life is as picture-perfect as it looks on social media. Even the happiest celebrity couple photo might have a pile of dirty laundry (literal or metaphorical) just out of frame.

In the end, one thing is clear across all these stories: love makes fools of us all, famous or not. Celebrities just get a bigger stage (and a louder audience) for their triumphs and mistakes. If there's any wisdom to glean from this parade of lovestruck lunacy, maybe it's this: Don't rush into multiple marriages with the same person expecting a different outcome. Don't treat finding a soulmate like a competitive reality show. Don't assume money or fame makes love any easier (it might just make it messier). And above all, don't buy the Instagram hype—behind every perfect grid is a real life that's at least a little chaotic.

The good news? We can laugh about it. Maybe not right in the thick of heartbreak, but give it time and even the craziest love fiascos become stories to tell (or lessons learned). The celebrity world just gives us a funhouse mirror to examine our own foibles. So go ahead, embrace the madness of love—just maybe do it with a bit more self-awareness than some of these folks. If Hollywood's finest can survive public scandals, divorces, and disaster dates and still stumble back into love again, there's hope for everyone. In the wild world of romance, we're all just trying our best, making mistakes, and occasionally looking ridiculous. And that, dear reader, is the beautifully human truth behind all the limelight lunacy.

Chapter 8

Swipe, Tap, Crash – Dating in the Digital Wild

Ghosts and Zombies: Modern Dating's Horror Show

Modern dating can feel like a Halloween special that never ends – full of ghosts and even the occasional zombie. Not the *Casper* or *Walking Dead* variety, of course, but the romantic kind. *Ghosting* – disappearing from someone's life without so much as a farewell GIF – has become shockingly common. In fact, a recent psychology survey found that a whopping 84% of Gen Z and millennials have been ghosted by someone they were dating. In other words, if you're a millennial or Gen Z single, odds are you've been on the receiving end of a digital vanishing act. Ghosting has "taken the world by storm" in relationships, and it extends beyond just flings – people even ghost friends and employers nowadays (one in four admit to ghosting a workplace!). It's a full-on haunt fest out there.

Why all the disappearing acts? Psychologists suggest a big reason is the lack of emotional accountability in modern app-based dating. When confronted with any discomfort or the urge to end things, many find it easier to simply *poof* – vanish – rather than have an honest conversation. The Thriving Center of Psychology study found that one of the main reasons people ghost is "they are no longer interested... and want to avoid confrontation". Essentially, conflict-avoidant ghosters slip away like digital phantoms instead of owning up to their feelings. It's an emotional hit-and-run, leaving the bewildered ghost-ee with no closure, just an eerie silence. Little wonder the most common reactions among the ghosted are *confusion, hurt, disappointment, and annoyance* – the romantic equivalent of staring into a void.

The emotional depth of some ghosters could be compared to a Snapchat filter: flashy and fun in the moment, but evaporating with a single tap. In the age of disappearing Stories, perhaps it's no surprise that disappearing people has become normalized. Ghosters often show as much sustained empathy as a 10-second vanishing Snap. One could say their sense of responsibility is as ephemeral as a bunny-ears filter – here one second, gone the next. And as a culture, we've oddly come to accept this. Three in four people now believe ghosting is acceptable in at least some situations. Talk about spooky: the bar for basic courtesy is six feet under.

But wait – like a late-night zombie film, just when you think the horror is over, it rises again. Enter "zombie-ing." If ghosting is the act of vanishing without a trace, zombie-ing is the sequel no one asked for: the ghost comes back from the dead. Suddenly, that person who disappeared from your texts weeks or months ago pops up again in your DMs saying *"Hey stranger… you up?"* as if nothing happened. (Braaaaains? More like draaaanks?) Refinery29 dryly defines it: "Zombieing is when someone ghosts you, but then decides to come back into your life like nothing happened." It adds insult to injury – as one commentator quipped, the zombie dater pretends you didn't just notice their weeks-long absence. The audacity! You're expected to carry on chatting as though they didn't pull a full disappearing act. It's the dating equivalent of a villain faking their own death and then strolling back in during the final chapter with a casual "Miss me?"

Culturally, ghosting and zombie-ing reflect a growing trend of low accountability and high emotional convenience. Why work through awkward conversations or admit loss of interest when you can just vanish, then later *resurrect* when lonely or bored? (Some experts note that boredom or seeking validation are indeed common motives for zombie-ing – the ghost misses their "source of entertainment" and wants to see if they can still get a reaction.) It's a horror show of emotional manners: the Ghoster has the transparency of a poltergeist, and the Zombie has the nerve of Frankenstein's monster asking for a date after rampaging the village.

Satirically speaking, the digital dating realm is like a haunted house. Ghosts glide through walls (or rather, block you on messaging apps) at the first sign of emotional depth. Zombies claw their way back with a cheery "Hey, been a minute!" text, expecting you to welcome them as if they didn't leave you in ghosted purgatory. Empathy often gets treated like an optional in-app purchase – one that many users skip. As one psychologist observed, ghosting is often a self-perpetuating cycle: people who get ghosted learn to ghost others as a twisted defense mechanism. Hurt people hurt people, or in this case, haunt people. The result is an entire generation of daters navigating a foggy graveyard of unresolved chat threads and phantom crushes.

And the effects aren't trivial. Being ghosted can genuinely sting, impacting self-esteem and trust. Some singles are so tired of the ghost-and-zombie carousel that 30% report feeling fed up with dating altogether in the past year. It's as if the dating pool is literally haunted – *who* has the energy to invest in a connection if it might end with the person disappearing into thin air? Meanwhile the ghosters themselves often feel it's the "easiest option" – many admit that when they ghost, they feel relief rather than remorse (a whopping 86% feel relief after ghosting someone!). That statistic alone speaks volumes about the emotional shallowness at play: guilt and accountability have left the chat, replaced by a sigh of relief and a shrug.

So in this modern dating horror show, we have a strange new norm: emotional exorcism. Ghosts drift among us on dating apps and text chats, cutting ties with all the tact of a disappearing Instagram Story. Zombies lurk too, ready to return from the dead whenever loneliness strikes, saying "boo" in your inbox as if that makes up for the vanishing act. It's absurd, it's prevalent, and it's setting the stage for the next chapter of digital dating absurdity. And speaking of stages, once you've dodged the ghosts and slammed the door on zombies, you then find yourself in another bizarre arena of modern love – one that looks less like a horror movie and more like a carnival of choices. Grab your popcorn (and your smartphone); it's time to enter the dating app buffet.

Dating App Déjà Vu

If surviving ghost stories wasn't enough, modern singles must also brave the endless buffet of dating apps. Think of dating apps as an all-you-can-swipe buffet: so many attractive options laid out, each profile a shiny tray of possibilities. In theory, it's a feast; in practice, you often walk away strangely unsatisfied (and a little queasy). This is the paradox of choice in action. Psychologist Barry Schwartz famously observed that too many options can lead to decision paralysis and dissatisfaction – and lo and behold, research has found the same in online dating. One study showed that participants who chose a date from a larger pool of options ended up less satisfied with their choice than those who picked from a smaller pool. With a seemingly infinite queue of profiles, it's easy to keep swiping in search of the Next Best Thing, never fully committing – the dating equivalent of taking a bite of every dessert at the buffet and savoring none.

At first, having *hundreds* of singles at your fingertips feels exciting – a thrill of abundance. You swipe, match, chat, like a kid in a candy store. But before long, the déjà vu sets in. Every profile starts to blur together into a stereotyped collage of hobbies and selfies. Here's a fun sampler of the ubiquitous profile clichés on these apps:

- **The World Traveler:** Poses at Machu Picchu or under a "Wanderlust" sign. Claims to "love adventure" and "seeking a partner in crime" for future trips (bonus points if they mention avocado toast in the same breath as backpacking – peak millennial energy).

- **The Fitness Buff:** At least one gym mirror selfie showing off those gains, or a hiking photo at sunrise. Apparently *everyone* on dating apps "loves hiking." If swipes translated to steps, we'd all be climbing Everest by now.

- **The Foodie/Brunch Aficionado:** Multiple pics of artfully arranged meals or them holding a quirky craft cocktail. Often accompanied by "I'm basically here for the tacos and good vibes." Yes, and presumably someone to photograph said tacos with.

- **The Pet Enthusiast:** Cuddling an adorable dog (who probably gets more right-swipes than the human). "Dog dad/mom looking for our third wheel." It's a cute play – who can say no to those puppy eyes? – but after the 50th profile, you start wondering if it's the same golden retriever making the rounds.

- **The Slightly Basic but Tries to Sound Unique:** Loves "adventures" (undefined), "work hard/play hard," "fluent in sarcasm," and is "equally comfortable in sweats or a tux/heels." Essentially, they just described 90% of the app's population. Groundbreaking.

After an hour of swiping, you might experience a strange sense of *been here, seen that*. The profiles all read from the same script, and you start getting the uncanny feeling you've matched with this person before – or at least their doppelgänger. This is dating app déjà vu: each new face seems eerily familiar due to the copy-paste personalities and photo tropes. It's as if everyone got the same memo that hiking, travel, gym selfies and avocado toast would make them stand out (when in fact they've made everyone blend in). The result? Swipe fatigue. Your swiping thumb gets tired, your eyes glaze over, and that exciting buffet now feels like picking at lukewarm leftovers.

It's not just you feeling this exhaustion. Studies confirm that the swipe frenzy is wearing people down. About 78% of dating app users report feeling "emotionally, mentally, or physically exhausted" by the experience. The endless stream of choices — and the disappointment when most matches lead nowhere — can be draining. It's paradoxical: having *more* options makes many of us *less* happy. Psychologists call it choice overload, and on dating apps it often translates into commitment-phobia and burnout. With an infinite menu of profiles, you worry that settling on one person means missing out on someone better who might be just one more swipe away. This buffet can give you a bad case of FOMO indigestion.

Another irony of the dating app buffet: even though we love to complain about how superficial or tiring these apps are, we're all still lining up at the buffet table. Online apps remain one of the most common places people meet partners in modern dating. So singles slog through the small talk and repetitive bios because, well, what's the alternative? Sure, your friend's cousin met their spouse while volunteering to rescue sea turtles, but for the rest of us mere mortals, it's back to Bumble on a Tuesday night, encountering the 17th profile in a row that says "I love The Office, tacos, and laughing until it hurts — if

you can't handle me at my worst, you don't deserve me at my best 😊 ."
(By the way, that Marilyn Monroe quote needs to be retired from dating
profiles. Please and thank you.)

The paradox of choice on apps also means that even when you do
get matches, conversations often fizzle out quickly. With so many
alternatives, people treat connections as disposable. Didn't reply in 5
minutes? On to the next chat. A minor awkward pause? Ghost and swipe
anew (thus feeding back into the ghosting culture). The buffet encourages
sampling without savoring. Many users report a sense of emptiness after
a while – the *Swipe, Match, Chat, Fade-out* cycle becomes as monotonous
as eating at the same chain restaurant every night. Everything starts to
taste the same.

And then there's the profile curation fatigue: trying to stand out
among millions of other buffeters. People agonize over which witty one-
liner or which travel photo will get them noticed. It's practically a second
job. Yet no matter how original you try to be, you fear coming off as
another cliché. (Spent a year in Asia finding yourself? Love your dog
more than life? So did the last ten profiles I saw.) The end result is a kind
of *dating app déjà vu* where both the shoppers and the goods feel eerily
indistinguishable.

Still, for all its absurdities, the dating app scene isn't going anywhere.
It truly is a buffet that many find themselves returning to, hoping that
this time the meal will be fulfilling. And sometimes it is – people do find
meaningful relationships there. But the process can be comically
repetitive and absurd. As one friend quipped, "Dating apps are where

optimism goes to die... and then respawn for another round." Swipe, swipe, yawn, repeat.

After navigating the spooky specters of ghosting and the dizzying buffet of swipe culture, one might hope that once you actually pair up with someone, the ride gets smoother. Think again. Now comes a peculiarly modern challenge for couples: the perilous world of text-message arguments. Yes, lovebirds, welcome to the era of fexting.

Fexting: Love in the Time of Typing

They say never go to bed angry – but what about never put down your phone angry? In our digital age, couples have taken their quarrels to the screens. Fexting – a portmanteau of "fighting + texting" – is the new way to argue in the 21st century. Instead of heated exchanges across the kitchen table, we now have dueling thumbs on tiny keyboards, firing off rapid retorts and *loaded* ellipsis bubbles. It's arguable (no pun intended) that fexting has become an epidemic of modern romance: According to one 2023 survey, 80% of people admit to arguing via text message with loved ones, rather than hashing it out face-to-face. Yep, eight in ten. The days of the classic shouting match are being replaced by the ping of an incoming iMessage at 1 a.m. saying "And another thing...".

Why are so many couples choosing to spar in text form? For one, it's *convenient*. You can battle from anywhere – no need to wait until you're both home; you can start a tiff while one of you is in a work meeting and the other is at the grocery store. It also feels *safer* in a way: you don't have to see the other person's face or hear their tone of voice. Conflict via text provides a buffer that some conflict-averse people prefer (echoes of ghosters avoiding confrontation). In fact, about half of fexting aficionados said they like it because texting gives them time to carefully consider their words – a chance to script the perfect zinger or measured response that they might fumble in person. It's conflict at arm's length.

But for all its perceived advantages, fexting is a treacherous endeavor. Sixty percent of people say that fighting via text has had a negative impact on their relationship. The reasons aren't hard to imagine. First, texting strips away all the nuance of human communication. *There's no vocal tone or body language in a text*, no matter how many emojis you tack on. As psychologists note, without tone of voice, it's "easy to assume the worst" about a message's intent. A sarcastic joke or a lightly teasing comment can come across as a cruel insult when seen in plain text with no context or intonation. ("Sure, you're *really* good at cleaning up 😑." Was that playful banter or an angry jab? Hard to tell over text, isn't it?) One person's harmless emoji can be another person's eye-roll from hell. A simple "K." reply can be interpreted as seething rage, passive-aggressive dismissal, or just brevity – and more often than not, it's assumed to be the worst option. In the absence of audible tone, our minds tend to fill in the blanks with thunderclouds.

Furthermore, texting encourages *rapid-fire response* in a way that can escalate conflict fast. The same survey found that about 30% of people respond to an angry text within 60 seconds – basically an emotional reflex. Instead of cooling off, taking a walk, or even pausing to count to ten, partners often impulsively thumb back a retort as soon as a hurtful message pops up. The result is an escalation – a flurry of messages flying back and forth, often with increasing length and intensity as each side tries to explain themselves or one-up the other. (Have you ever sent a paragraph-long text in an argument, only to get a one-word reply? Cue *more* anger.) Indeed, research suggests that text spats tend to drag out longer than in-person arguments – nearly 60% of people said *fexting actually prolongs the fight* compared to if they talked in person. All those clarifications, screenshots of past messages ("See, you *did* say that last week!"), and perfectly composed rebuttals keep the argument simmering far longer than a face-to-face quarrel might.

Another pitfall: *receipts.* Texting creates a written log of your fight. In the heat of anger, couples may lob harsh words that, once on screen, can be saved, scrolled, and re-read obsessively – either by the couple themselves (reliving the anger) or, catastrophically, by others if one partner shows screenshots to a friend for sympathy. In an in-person spat, harsh words disappear into the air; in a text fight, that snarky comment about your mother-in-law's lasagna is immortalized. This can make forgiveness harder. As one therapist put it, when you argue in person, you eventually cool off and move on; but in text, "you can scroll back up and relive the argument" over and over. It's the fight that never dies – basically the zombie-ing of arguments.

Miscommunication is practically the default setting of fexting. Without body language or immediate feedback, messages are easily misread. You might think you're making a rational point, but your partner perceives a different tone entirely. And because you can't see their furrowed brow or hear the quiver in their voice, you might not realize how upset they are becoming. As a result, things can "escalate to a terrible point without one person even becoming aware how upset the other is," notes one relationship expert. By the time you realize how badly you've both misunderstood each other, feelings have been deeply hurt – all via a device typically used to send smiley faces and memes.

To add a layer of comedy to the tragedy, consider the emoji battles that happen mid-fight. One person sends 🙃 (upside-down smile) – is that an olive branch or mild annoyance? The other fires back with 😤 (steam from nose) – or wait, was that intended as determination? When words fail, couples sometimes start flinging emojis like modern hieroglyphics of anger. It would be hilarious if it weren't so commonplace. "We argued about whether the poop emoji I sent was *literal* or *figurative*," one might say sheepishly. Yes, this is love in the time of typing: where even a pile of poo can become a point of contention.

All joking aside, fexting is widely acknowledged as problematic for relationships. Even Jill Biden – the First Lady of the US – admitted that she and President Biden occasionally "fext" (fight over text) and that he once responded, "You realize that's going to go down in history. There will be a record of that" (wise words, Mr. President). While fexting might feel easier in the moment (no awkward confrontations or risk of shouting), it often leads to *more* misunderstandings than it resolves. Many relationship experts caution that important or emotionally charged conversations should be held in person or at least via voice, where you can hear tone and interact in real time. A tiny phone screen is simply too small to contain the big emotions of love and conflict.

Unfortunately, breaking the fexting habit can be tough. Our phones are always with us, tempting us to air grievances the instant they arise. Patience is in short supply. Why wait when you can send a scathing text novella *right now* and perhaps get the catharsis of seeing those three little typing dots appear, indicating you've provoked a response? It's a trap many fall into. And so, modern couples find themselves in this absurd situation: sitting in separate rooms (or separate offices, or separate cities), furiously typing and turning what used to be a spoken spat into a prolonged email-length exchange that could be titled "War and Peace: iMessage Edition."

In the end, most would agree that fexting is a lose-lose. You miss the chance to truly hear and see each other, and you gain a whole lot of confusion and hurt. Perhaps the only "win" is for the autocorrect comedy gods (turning your "I'm mad as hell" into "I'm mad at shell" and momentarily defusing tension with absurdity). For the health of relationships, though, many are learning to put down the phone and discuss serious matters face-to-face – or at least via a video call if long-distance. Speaking of which, not all modern digital romance woes involve conflict; some involve *distance*. And that brings us to our final act in this saga: the long-distance relationship in an era of hyper-connectivity.

Long-Distance in the 5G Era

It's a classic irony of our hyper-connected age: we have 5G internet, instant video calls, and real-time everything, yet long-distance relationships (LDRs) can still feel *achingly* long-distance. On one hand, today's technology makes it easier than ever to maintain a relationship across miles. We don't have to wait weeks for a love letter carried by pigeon or pony express; we can send an "I miss you" text that lights up our partner's phone on the other side of the world in milliseconds. We fall asleep on video calls with our far-away beloved, binge Netflix together via Telepathy, and spend weekends having virtual dinner dates – each of us dining solo, laptop propped up so we can see each other chew and chat. In theory, being apart has never been more bearable. In practice, it's a strange mix of *charm* and *challenge*.

The charm is easy to see. Technology allows couples to bridge gaps that previous generations couldn't. Got an ocean between you? No problem – hop on Zoom or FaceTime and you can gaze into each other's eyes nightly without hefty phone bills (thank goodness video calls are basically free now). Want to watch a movie "together" though you're 500 miles apart? Stream it simultaneously and text or voice-chat throughout; it's almost like you're on the same couch (minus the popcorn sharing). During the pandemic, many couples even had entire dates on Zoom, getting dressed up for a virtual dinner or cooking together from afar. There are stories of people falling in love via long-distance video calls when travel was shut down. And for those of a geekier persuasion, virtual reality meet-ups are a thing: apparently LDR couples have met up in VR spaces to simulate walks in the park or even attend virtual concerts together. We truly live in the future.

Thanks to these innovations, some long-distance couples actually communicate more than couples who live in the same city. It's counterintuitive but true – studies note that increased communication frequency in LDRs has become commonplace with quick check-in texts, constant availability, etc. In fact, some LDR partners "communicate more frequently than local couples" because it's so easy to ping each other throughout the day. Many fall into an "always-on" pattern: since your phone is always on you, and your loved one is just a message away, there's an unspoken expectation to stay in touch nearly 24/7. Especially early on, this can feel intoxicating – you're texting, calling, sending memes and updates constantly. Your phone buzzes and it's them, and your heart skips – it's like a permanent state of romantic dopamine hit. Being *that* connected, even while apart, can give a giddy sense of closeness.

But then comes the flip side: digital dependency. The same connectivity that keeps you bonded can start to feel like a lifeline you're terrified to let go of. LDR couples may find that they *have* to text "Good morning" and "Good night" every single day, or one of them feels abandoned. If an hour goes by without a reply, anxiety creeps in. ("He usually texts during lunch… is something wrong? Is he dead? Did he meet someone new in the last 57 minutes?") It sounds neurotic, but it happens. Experts note that for some, overreliance on digital tools leads to feeling *more* disconnected whenever the phone goes silent – as if your relationship lives in the phone, and when the phone is off, the relationship is on pause. You risk developing the unsettling sense that you're "living online rather than in person." You might even start to panic if you haven't gotten a text in a while. The line between healthy contact and obsessive constant contact can get blurry when your partner isn't physically present to remind you they're still there in the world.

Psychologically, this can take a toll. You're always semi-available to each other, which can be both comfort and burden. Yes, it's lovely to know your partner is one video call away, but it also means you might feel guilty if you just want a night *off* from the screen. Long-distance pairs often schedule virtual date nights and constant communication to compensate for distance, but it can start to feel like a part-time job. One partner might secretly think, "I'd love to just read a book tonight without narrating my every thought to you," but worry that pulling back would weaken the bond. The *charm* of digital closeness comes hand-in-hand with the *challenge* of digital dependence.

Another hidden strain: Zoom fatigue, romantic edition. It turns out video calls can be surprisingly draining. Studies during the pandemic found that video chats actually require more energy and focus than face-to-face interactions, often leaving people feeling *more* exhausted and even lonelier. There's something slightly artificial about staring at a pixelated rendering of your partner's face, trying to glean genuine connection through a screen. As wonderful as it is to see and hear them in real time, it can also heighten the awareness of the distance. Researchers noted that many people in long-distance situations reported that long video calls, while essential, sometimes reminded them *"how far away that person was and how long it would be until they got to hold them again"*. It's heartbreaking in a way – the call ends and you're left with a silent room and the ache of their absence. In the 5G era, you can connect anytime, but that doesn't magically erase the miles; sometimes it highlights them.

The digital nature of communication can also introduce *new* types of misunderstandings. Much like fexting, pure text-based long-distance communication can misfire. Even frequent video calls, as noted, lack the full warmth of physical presence. Couples might struggle with maintaining intimacy through a screen – no amount of heart emojis can fully replace a hug. There's even the phenomenon of the "illusion of intimacy": feeling emotionally very close through texts and talks, but when you finally reunite in person, it's a bit awkward at first. You have to recalibrate to physical togetherness, which can be jarring ("Oh, you're taller than you look on FaceTime!"). Many an LDR couple has had that mildly disconcerting moment when their reunion feels like meeting a well-known stranger.

And yet, many long-distance couples *thrive*. They often develop superb communication habits – talking for hours, really delving into each other's thoughts and feelings, because that's all they have. Some research even suggests LDR couples can build stronger emotional bonds and clarity about their relationship because they spend so much time talking (all you *do* is talk, talk, talk). They don't take time together for granted, and when they do reunite, it's fireworks. The hyper-connected nature of our era, for all its pitfalls, at least gives these couples a fighting chance. Imagine doing long-distance in the 1970s: one pricey long-distance call a week and maybe some letters. Today, you can virtually live in your partner's pocket via messaging apps and live video. It's both a blessing and a bizarre simulation of togetherness.

In a satirical sense, the 5G long-distance romance is almost like having a digital twin of your partner. You interact with their digital avatar (their texts, their video presence) daily, while the 3D flesh-and-blood version is elsewhere. Your relationship exists in a cloud, literally. You celebrate anniversaries on Zoom. You fall asleep on call, joking that the snoring in your headphones is kinda cute. You become connoisseurs of virtual date ideas: "Tonight, let's tour the Louvre together on Street View," or "How about we both order pepperoni pizza and have a Skype picnic?" It's equal parts adorable and absurd. Modern problems do inspire modern solutions – some LDR couples send touch bracelets or WiFi-connected pillows that glow or vibrate when the other person hugs theirs, so you can *feel* a virtual hug. Is it cheesy? Absolutely. Does it warm the heart? Perhaps a bit, if you're love-drunk enough.

Ultimately, long-distance in the digital age is a testament to human adaptability. Love finds a way – through fiber optic cables, through cellphone towers, through whatever medium it can. The experience is a mix of irony and earnestness. It's ironic that we have Star Trek-level communication tech yet still yearn and ache as much as ever. It's charming that two people can maintain a flame across continents by the glow of their screens. It's absurd that a bad Wi-Fi connection can cause tears because the video call dropped right when you were about to say "I love you." It's the new normal that being glued to your phone is a sign of devotion, not disengagement, when your sweetheart lives far away.

As our narrator closes this chapter on modern digital dating, one can't help but marvel (and chuckle) at how love and courtship have evolved.

We have ghost stories where the ghosts are very much alive (just commitment-phobic), dating smorgasbords that leave us both overstuffed and empty, text wars fought with furious thumbs, and love affairs sustained by satellites and data packets. It's a wild world, equal parts ridiculous and relatable. Through it all, the human desire for connection remains the same – we just express it now through swipes, snaps, texts, and video chats. In the grand story of love, this era might be a comedic chapter, full of quirks and cringe, but also creativity and hope. After all, if couples can survive *that* argument over the meaning of a smiley emoji, or sustain passion through a pixelated screen, maybe they can survive anything. Modern digital dating may be complex and absurd, but it's the reality we navigate – one ghost, swipe, and text at a time.

And who knows? Perhaps the next innovation will finally solve some of these woes – a sarcasm font to prevent text misunderstandings, a teleportation device for LDR date nights, an AI that gently reminds ghosters to send a polite breakup text instead of vanishing. Until then, we persevere, finding humor in the chaos and comfort in knowing we're all in this crazy digital love boat together. Bon appétit and good luck out there – just don't get zombied.

Chapter 9

The Love Lab – Science of the Heart (and Other Organs)

Welcome to the Love Lab, where we put romance under a microscope (figuratively—no hearts were harmed in the making of this chapter). Love might feel magical, but behind those butterflies and heart-eye emojis is a wild chemical circus in your body. In this chapter, we'll dissect the science of love with a wink and a laugh, exploring how falling head-over-heels can hijack your brain like a drug, why your organs (yes, other than your heart) go haywire when you're smitten, and how our childhood wiring can turn us into clingy koalas or lone wolves in love. We'll even see why a lover's quarrel can feel as scary as a bear attack until a simple hug works like a peace treaty. Strap on your safety goggles (and maybe grab some chocolate for research purposes) – class is in session in the Love Lab!

Your Brain on Love: Addicted from the First Kiss

Ever notice how falling in love can make you act a *little* crazy? You're grinning at your phone like a goofball, daydreaming mid-meeting, maybe even doodling your crush's name with hearts around it. (If you've ever carved initials into a tree, don't worry – that tree forgives you.) There's a scientific reason new love turns even rational people into obsessed fools. Neuroscientists have found that romantic love hijacks your brain's reward circuitry much like an addictive drug does. In fact, the same regions of the brain that light up for a cocaine high are activated when you gaze at your beloved. The first kiss alone can trigger a *rush* of dopamine – the feel-good neurotransmitter – hitting the brain's pleasure center and leaving you craving more, just like a junkie chasing the next hit. It's as if nature slipped a love potion into your neurochemistry, turning you into an addict for affection from that very first smooch.

Dopamine is the star of this show – it's the chemical that surges during infatuation and makes everything about that person seem *incredibly* fascinating. Remember the euphoria of having a crush reciprocate your feelings? That's dopamine flooding your brain's reward system, giving you a natural high. Suddenly you have boundless energy, need less sleep, and can't stop thinking about them. (Those 2 A.M. deep chats when you both have work the next day? Blame dopamine.) One quirky study even showed that male fruit flies, when sexually rejected, would drown their sorrows in alcohol – they drank four times more booze than those who had mated, apparently seeking an alternate reward since love let them down. Same reward center at work, different method of getting buzzed! If even fruit flies turn to *love on the rocks* (literally) after a breakup, what chance do we humans have against the allure of love's high?

But dopamine doesn't party alone. When Cupid's arrow strikes, other brain chemicals join the fiesta. Early-stage love sees a spike in norepinephrine (a cousin of adrenaline), which makes your heart race and palms sweat as if you're in a thrilling chase. (That jittery excitement when you get a text from *you-know-who*? That's basically your brain doing a happy dance.) At the same time, something peculiar happens: levels of serotonin, a neurotransmitter linked to mood and stability, can drop during infatuation. Low serotonin is linked to obsessive-compulsive tendencies – and indeed, those first weeks of love can feel like a delightful *OCD*: you have intrusive, maddeningly preoccupying thoughts about the person nonstop. Ever caught yourself re-reading old messages 50 times or replaying your last conversation on a loop? That's infatuation behaving a bit like a mental obsession. One scientist described early love as a form of "temporary insanity" – and honestly, who are we to argue when we've all seen otherwise sensible people compose cringey love poems at 3 AM or consider driving 100 miles just to see someone for an hour?

Even our critical thinking takes a backseat. Brain scans of people in love have shown reduced activity in the areas responsible for negative judgment and social critique. In other words, love *literally* makes us more blind to red flags and flaws – the neural basis for the old saying "love is blind". That's why you might overlook the fact that your new partner leaves dirty dishes everywhere or has a questionable fondness for karaoke nights; your brain's alarm system for others' faults is sedated by love. (Friends on the outside looking in are facepalming, but you're floating on cloud nine without a cloud of judgment in sight.)

All these brain changes mean that falling in love is a full-body experience as potent as any drug. It can happen astonishingly fast, too – one study suggests it takes only about one-fifth of a second to fall in love. (Speedrunners, eat your heart out!) That explains the classic movie trope of "love at first sight": biologically, your brain can be *addicted at first kiss.* And once it's hooked, you're effectively a lab rat pressing the lever for more dopamine treats. You'll find yourself doing delightfully ridiculous things to keep the high going: smiling at your phone like an idiot (thanks oxytocin, we'll get to you soon), replaying that goofy voicemail just to hear their voice, or yes, carving your initials into a tree like you're starring in a 1980s rom-com. It's not *rational*, but neither is snorting cocaine – and in the brain's reward pathways, love and drugs aren't so different. No wonder we say we're "addicted" to a person or "drunk" in love (cheers to you, Beyoncé, for that apt metaphor).

Of course, Mother Nature isn't just trying to make fools of us for fun – there's an evolutionary method to this madness. The brain's reward circuit (which evolved to reinforce survival behaviors like eating and procreating) treats romantic love like a prize to be chased. That intense focus on one person helped our ancestors form bonds and stick together to raise babies. It's hard to flake on your partner when your brain is literally *hooked* on them. So if you feel like a love-struck fool acting out of character, cut yourself some slack: it's your ancient lizard brain working to secure a mate, by any means necessary. (Obsessive gushing and late-night serenades included.)

Before we move on, a comforting note: this crazed, love-drunk state isn't permanent (phew!). Studies suggest that after about 12-24 months, the initial fire cools and your brain regains some chill. The dopamine frenzy subsides to more sustainable levels, serotonin creeps back to normal (so you can finally concentrate on work again), and love moves into a calmer, long-term attachment phase. In essence, the rollercoaster evens out. But while it lasts, enjoy the ride – there's nothing quite like that first-kiss high, and now you know your brain is *literally* under the influence. Just maybe refrain from any permanent tattoos of your new lover's name during this phase, okay?

Transition: Speaking of being under the influence, let's take a closer look at the chemicals coursing through your veins when love strikes. We've mentioned dopamine and serotonin; they're just two members of love's chemical boy band. It's time to meet the rest of the crew – the hormones tugging at your heartstrings (and yes, other organs) when you're swooning.

Hormones and Heartstrings

When you fall in love, your body basically brews up a potent love cocktail that affects everything from your brain to your gut. Consider this your cocktail menu of the four key "ingredients" in love's potion: dopamine, oxytocin, adrenaline, and cortisol. Each chemical comes with its own outrageous effects – from sweaty palms and racing hearts to warm fuzzy cuddles. Let's break down the biochemical cast of characters (with a twist of humor):

- **Dopamine – The Pleasure Potion:** Dopamine is the headliner of the love cocktail, the same neurotransmitter that gives a runner's high or a gambler's thrill. In romance, it's the *giddy elixir* of euphoria. Dopamine is released in brain regions linked to reward and motivation, making you feel exhilarated and laser-focused on your partner. It's why new love can feel *so good* it's addictive. Ever notice how everything reminds you of your beloved when you're high on dopamine? A love song on the radio, a random billboard, even a jar of peanut butter – they all somehow connect to *them*. You can thank dopamine for that *phenomenal cosmic focus* (and for those late-night bursts of energy when you should be exhausted). In pop culture terms, dopamine is the reason sitcom characters do wild things for love – like Ted Mosby stealing a blue French horn for Robin on *How I Met Your Mother*. It's the brain's way of saying "Go get 'em, tiger!" and rewarding you for every romantic gesture.

- **Oxytocin – The Cuddle Chemical:** Oxytocin is often nicknamed the "love hormone" or "cuddle hormone," and for good reason. It's released during physical touch – hugs, holding hands, snuggling on the couch, and certainly during sex. If dopamine is the fireworks of infatuation, oxytocin is the gentle candlelight that follows. It deepens feelings of attachment and trust, giving you those warm, content, "I feel so safe with you" vibes. When you curl up with your sweetheart to watch Netflix and feel like all's right in the world, that's oxytocin flooding your system, lowering stress and ushering in calm and security. Oxytocin is also the peacemaker; it's released when you kiss and make up after a fight, helping to cement your bond. (Fun fact: it's the same hormone that bonds mothers to babies during breastfeeding – talk about strong stuff!). Think of oxytocin as the heartstring tie – each affectionate touch is like clicking "Save" on the relationship, reinforcing that emotional connection. No wonder a good long hug can melt away anger; one study found that a simple hug can trigger beneficial physiological changes, reducing stress and boosting mood via oxytocin release. It's basically a *free* anti-anxiety drug in hormone form – which might explain why so many rom-coms end with a comforting embrace.

- **Adrenaline (Epinephrine) –** The Spark Plug: Adrenaline is the hormone behind your pounding heart, sweaty palms, and butterfly-filled stomach in the early stages of love. It's part of the body's arousal system – the same "fight or flight" chemical that would surge if you were, say, being chased by a bear... or, somewhat similarly, about to lean in for a first kiss. That first-date jitteriness and slight breathlessness? Classic adrenaline rush. In fact, researchers have noted that falling in love triggers a release of adrenaline (and its sidekick norepinephrine) along with the dopamine, effectively putting your body on high alert. Blood vessels dilate to send more oxygen around (hence those flushed cheeks), your pupils may dilate (making that smoldering eye contact even more intense), and you might even feel a little shaky on your feet. (Ever gone weak in the knees when kissed? You're not imagining it – that's adrenaline spiking in your brain.) Evolutionarily, this makes sense: meeting a potential mate is *important*, so your body reacts as if something crucial is happening (which, from a genes perspective, it is!). The humorous downside is that adrenaline doesn't discriminate between *good* excitement and sheer terror. So your body basically acts like a thrilled, panicked mess whether you're on the most amazing date of your life or accidentally butt-dialing your boss – racing heart, trembling hands, the works. Many a romantic comedy has milked this for laughs: think of every awkward love confession scene where someone is stammering and sweating bullets. Blame adrenaline for making love as physically intense as a high-speed chase (with hopefully less actual danger).

- **Cortisol – The Stress Hormone:** Cortisol is usually thought of as the stress chemical – it's released by your adrenal glands in times of pressure or conflict. Surprise! It shows up in romance too, especially in the *early* phase of love. When you first fall for someone, your cortisol levels actually increase, as if your body thinks being in love is a kind of stressor. And in a way, it is – it's a *good* stress, but your body is still like "Whoa, something big is happening, mobilize resources!" Elevated cortisol in new love might give you that keyed-up feeling: you're excited but also anxious, euphoric but also jittery, almost like you're bracing for a "crisis". (It *is* kind of a life-altering event for your brain, after all.) Cortisol is a bit of a double agent in the love saga. In small doses, it helps rally your energy and focus – you're on your toes, your immune system even gets a little boost, you feel *alive*. But too much for too long can fry your nerves. Over time, as a relationship stabilizes, cortisol should drop back down to normal, which is why long-term love feels more like a safe haven than a rollercoaster. Yet cortisol doesn't disappear from the love story; it re-emerges during relationship conflicts. Have a heated argument with your partner, and bam – cortisol surges again, flooding you with stress. (So *that's* why your heart is still hammering an hour after arguing about whose turn it is to take out the trash.) We'll see more about cortisol in conflict in the next section, but for now remember: this hormone wears two hats. In passion, cortisol is the *flaming hot sauce* that spices things up with urgency; in conflict, it's the bitter medicine that makes your chest tight and your mood tank. Truly, cortisol is the drama queen of hormones – stirring the pot in love and war alike.

With this quartet of chemicals playing in concert, it's no wonder love is such a full-body symphony. Your heart races and palms sweat when you're falling headlong for someone because adrenaline and cortisol are literally mimicking a stress response (very convenient when you're trying to act cool on a date, right?). Meanwhile, the euphoria and giddiness come from dopamine setting off fireworks in your brain's pleasure centers, akin to the rush of sugar or narcotics (love might be the only legal drug that comes baked into our biology). And the warm fuzzies and contentment? Credit oxytocin, flooding you with calm after the storm, making you want to cuddle and stay close.

Consider a typical rom-com storyline: Two characters meet (cue *adrenaline* and *dopamine* as they flirt awkwardly at first, hearts pounding). Montage of blissful dates (dopamine continues to spike – they're basically high on each other). Then comes the misunderstanding or fight (cortisol and adrenaline up again – stress, tears, maybe a dramatic airport chase scene fueled by panic). Finally, the reconciliation kiss (a wave of oxytocin and dopamine washes over them – calm, joyous relief as music swells). Science has basically scripted every rom-com ever, with hormones as the ghostwriters.

One more fascinating aspect: over time, the balance of these chemicals shifts. The crazy adrenaline/dopamine cocktail of early love gradually gives way to a steadier brew heavy on oxytocin (and its lesser-known partner, vasopressin, which supports long-term bonding and monogamy). This is why the passion transforms into deeper attachment as couples hit their stride. It's not that the love is less real – it's that your body moves from a fiery sprint to a marathon pace. The "honeymoon phase" truly is a biological phase. And while some might miss the butterflies and manic excitement, the trade-off is worth it: you get a love that can actually let you sleep at night and eat full meals without your stomach being in knots. (Ah, stability – so underrated when you're no longer a dopamine junkie.)

In summary, love strings your heart along via hormones that can make you feel ecstatic, anxious, energized, and cozy all at once. It's the most complex, exquisite chemical high there is. Just remember when your heartstrings are tugged and your pulse is thumping: that's your body's way of saying "this person *matters*." Evolution cooked up this cocktail to push us into each other's arms – and sometimes, to keep us there through the storms. And speaking of storms, what happens when those warm fuzzy feelings give way to conflict? Before we get there, we need to talk about one more piece of the puzzle: how your personal attachment style (basically, your relationship *personality*) interacts with all these hormones to produce either smooth sailing or perfect storms in love.

Attachment Styles: Clingers, Avoiders, and Secure Unicorns

Not everyone rides the love rollercoaster the same way. Some of us scream and hold on for dear life (the Clingers), some prefer the kiddie rides and keep distance (the Avoiders), and a lucky few seem to enjoy the ride with a serene smile and barf-free experience (the Secure, aka those mythical unicorns of healthy romance). These patterns are known as attachment styles – basically, your default setting for how you connect with others emotionally. The concept comes from psychology research: originally from John Bowlby's studies of how infants attach to caregivers, later extended to adult love by researchers like Cindy Hazan and Philip Shaver. Your attachment style is shaped by early experiences (like how your parents responded to you) and, it turns out, it can heavily influence your love life. Don't worry, we're not diving into a dry therapy textbook here – we'll keep it fun. Let's explore these styles as if they were *dating archetypes* you might recognize in yourself, your friends, or sitcom characters:

- **Clingers (Anxious Attachment):** These are the folks who love *hard* and fear losing it. If you're a Clinger, you crave closeness and reassurance like it's oxygen. You might text your partner throughout the day ("just checking in again!"), overanalyze their every emoji, and feel on edge if they take a few hours to reply. Psychologists call this anxious or ambivalent attachment. It often traces back to inconsistent caregiving in childhood – never being sure if love will be available, so as an adult you're hyper-vigilant about any sign of distancing. In pop culture, think of *Ross Geller*

159

from Friends when he got jealous and paranoid about Rachel – classic anxious moves (we all remember the infamous "we were on a break" meltdown). Or that one ex who sent 20 unanswered texts in a row when you were in a meeting – yep, that energy. On the positive side, Clingers are very loving and loyal, always willing to work for the relationship. But they can become *overly* fixated on the relationship's status. A Clinger in full panic mode might say things like, "Do you still love me? You hesitated when I asked, is something wrong?!" They might interpret a partner's need for a night out with friends as an ominous sign. It's exhausting being in their head, trust me. In scientific studies, about 19–20% of adults tend toward this anxious style. These individuals often worry their partner will abandon them or doesn't love them enough, which can lead to behaviors like clinging tighter when they sense distance. Picture a koala hugging a tree for dear life – except the tree is an understandably perplexed partner. The irony is that the more a Clinger pursues ("I need to hear you love me for the 5th time today"), the more an Avoider partner (we'll meet them next) might want to flee, setting up a frustrating cycle. The good news is, with communication and self-soothing (and often a partner who offers lots of reassurance), anxious individuals can feel more secure. And hey, at least you'll never be accused of not caring enough!

- **Avoiders (Avoidant Attachment):** These are the independent souls, the lone wolves who value their space *a lot*. If commitment-phobes had a mascot, it would be the Avoider. People with avoidant attachment can certainly fall in love, but intimacy often makes them uncomfortable after a certain point. They pull back when things get too close or when they feel a partner's expectations mounting. Ever dated someone who ghosted for a day or two after a deep conversation, or who joked that they're "allergic to cuddling"? That's Avoider vibes. Psychologically, avoidant attachment often develops when caregivers were emotionally distant or when independence was emphasized early on. As adults, Avoiders tend to avoid deep emotional involvement as a protective measure – they often pride themselves on not *needing* others too much. A classic Avoider line might be, "I'm not ready for anything serious" or "I need a lot of *me-time*, it's just how I am." On TV, James Bond (though not a sitcom character) is an archetypal Avoider – charming and passionate in the moment, but always flying solo into the sunset. Or consider Robin Scherbatsky from *How I Met Your Mother*: she hated the idea of commitment and kids, and would emotionally distance when Ted got too close. Avoiders can come off as cool and confident, but inside they often wrestle with discomfort about depending on someone. Roughly 25% of adults are thought to have an avoidant style. They often **fear closeness and think they don't really need love to be happy】 – at least that's the story they tell themselves. In reality, of course, avoidant folks *do* desire love; they just get *overwhelmed* by it. Their strategy in relationships is often to put up walls or create distance when vulnerability looms. For example, an Avoider might choose work, hobbies, or solo travel over spending extra quality time with a partner, especially if the relationship is getting serious. To a Clinger partner, this feels like cold rejection ("Why does he want to go on a week-long hiking trip without me?!"). But to the Avoider, it's a way to regulate their fear of dependence. Pop culture is full of jokes about commitment-phobic bachelors or bachelorettes – those are our Avoiders in a nutshell. Yet, not all hope is lost: Avoiders can and do form lasting relationships, especially with understanding partners who give them space while gradually building trust. With time, even a lone wolf can learn that letting someone in won't necessarily lead to losing oneself. (Cue the heartfelt scene where the Avoider finally admits, "I... I need you," and everyone watching the rom-com cheers.)

- **Secure (The Secure Unicorns):** Ah, the Secure attachment folks – truly the unicorns of the dating world. About 50–60% of people thankfully are secure, though in the drama of life they sometimes feel as rare as unicorns because, well, they don't cause as much drama! A securely attached person is comfortable with intimacy and independence. They communicate their needs openly and calmly, and they respond to their partner's needs reliably. If you're secure, you're not perfect (no one is), but you likely don't obsess over every text or freak out when your partner has a night out. You trust that you're loved and that if issues arise, you can talk them through. Psychologists say this comes from having had reasonably responsive, reliable caregiving in childhood – basically, you learned early on that people are trustworthy and love doesn't always bite. In a relationship, Secures tend to be the *stable glues*. They can manage conflict without the world ending, and they can give and receive affection without losing their sense of self. Imagine a couple that actually discusses feelings openly, listens to each other, and makes each other feel safe – *gasp!* Yes, it exists. Think Pam and Jim from *The Office* – their relationship had its humorous ups and downs, but at core it was supportive, understanding, and based on friendship (pretty darn secure). Or many of the steady couples in the background of shows – they don't get the spotlight because they're not a hot mess, but they're relationship goals. Being with a Secure person feels like a warm blanket for your heart: you don't have to guess how they feel, and you don't fear they'll bolt at the slightest issue. They engage in what experts call "effective communication and healthy interdependence" – in plain terms, they can need someone without being needy, and be relied on without feeling burdened. It's almost *boring* how healthy they are, which ironically is incredibly attractive when you're used to rollercoasters. The term "unicorn" is a playful jab at how elusive this can seem if you've been dating a string of Clingers and Avoiders, but fear not: Secures are out there, living proof that not every romance is doomed to chaos. In fact, attachment research shows that secure attachment *can be learned* or earned over time. For example, an anxiously attached person can become more secure if they date someone who consistently shows them love and reliability (essentially rewiring their expectations). Likewise, an Avoider can thaw out in the steady warmth of a secure partner who doesn't push too hard or abandon them. So unicorns can, it seems, share their magic. Many of us start out as one of the insecure types and gradually become more secure as we grow and find better relationship patterns. That's the hope, anyway – and science backs it up. Meanwhile, if you are a Secure unicorn reading this, thank you for your service; you give the rest of us hope and a role model for what *sane and happy love* can look like!

It's important to note that these styles aren't boxes to trap people in, but more like tendencies on a spectrum. You might find you have a mix of anxious and secure traits, or you're mostly secure but turn avoidant under stress, etc. And attachment styles can change with experiences – a bad breakup might make even a secure person act a bit more clingy next time, or a great partner might help an anxious person chill out. But it's pretty wild (and useful) how accurately these categories explain a lot of relationship behaviors. Suddenly, your ex who always pulled away makes sense (Avoider!), and your friend who serial-texts paragraphs to their crush fits a pattern (Clinger alert!).

Understanding these styles can be liberating and even humorous. We can laugh at ourselves a bit: "Haha, there I was, freaking out that my partner didn't use an exclamation mark in their text – classic anxious me." Or "Oops, I spent 5 hours gaming instead of calling her back – avoidant much?" It's like discovering your internal relationship software. And once you know your "programming," you can hack it for the better. The anxious can learn to self-soothe ("Alright brain, no, them taking a spa day doesn't mean they're leaving me") and communicate needs without panic. The avoidant can practice opening up in small doses ("Maybe I'll share this feeling rather than retreat into my man-cave for a week"). The secure can help their less secure partners feel safe by being consistent and empathetic.

One more cool thing: attachment styles don't just affect how we behave, they even tie back to our biochemistry under the hood. For instance, studies have found that anxiously attached individuals tend to have a stronger cortisol stress response when they even *anticipate* conflict with their partner. It's like their body hits the panic button faster – heart rate up, stress hormones flooding – because the thought of relationship trouble is extra scary to them. Avoidant folks, on the other hand, might show a blunted stress response; they often *physically* keep cool during conflict, which sounds nice except it might be because they're disconnecting emotionally (their cortisol doesn't surge as much since they're busy emotionally checking out). So if you've ever marveled at how one person in a couple is red-faced and yelling while the other is icily calm, attachment science might say: anxious vs. avoidant in action, literally down to their adrenal glands. Talk about mind-body connection!

Alright, now we know our love personality types and the chemical soup we're swimming in. What happens when love isn't all candlelight and roses? Every couple, no matter how compatible, eventually faces conflict – from minor tiffs to major blow-outs. Time to address the messy part of love: fights and the biological fight-or-flight response that comes with them. Why do we sometimes react to a lover's quarrel like it's a life-

or-death battle, and how can understanding our inner caveperson help us cool down and make up? Step back into the Love Lab arena – things might get a bit heated (but don't worry, we'll end with a hug).

Fight, Flight, or Make Up

Picture this: You're in the middle of a heated argument with your partner about, oh, let's say leaving the wet towels on the floor. Hardly a saber-tooth tiger attack, right? And yet, your heart is thumping, your face is flushed, your muscles are tense, and you feel a bead of sweat forming as if you're in danger. Meanwhile, your partner's voice starts sounding oddly like a growl to your brain. Congratulations – you're experiencing a fight-or-flight response in the midst of domestic bliss! As absurd as it seems, our bodies can react to relationship conflict just like they would to an actual threat. Evolutionarily, conflict with our significant other *is* a threat – not to our immediate survival perhaps, but to our deep need for social connection and security. So when bae raises their voice, your ancient brain might genuinely process it like "Bear attack! Sound the alarms!" 😱.

What's going on under the hood is that the amygdala, the fear center of your brain (fondly nicknamed here as the "Mad-Eye Moody" of the brain for its constant vigilance), has detected a threat in your environment – in this case, an *angry loved one*. It doesn't matter that this threat is a harsh tone about towels and not, say, a predator; the amygdala is not exactly a master of nuance. It fires off an alarm, and instantly your body is flooded with stress hormones, primarily adrenaline and cortisol – our old friends from earlier, but now deployed for battle. Your heart races, muscles tense, digestion slows, pupils widen – classic sympathetic nervous system activation to prep you to either fight the "enemy" or flee the scene. This happens *before* your conscious thought kicks in. That's why you might blurt out something nasty or get defensive in a split-second; your logical brain (the prefrontal cortex) literally got bypassed when the amygdala hit the panic button. In short, when tempers flare, you go caveman: body ready to throw down or run, and higher reasoning on a coffee break.

For example, say your partner yells, "You never listen to me!" In a microsecond, your pulse jumps. Internally, one part of you is now poised to either fight ("Oh yeah? Well *you* never wash the dishes!") or take flight ("I'm out of here, I can't deal with this."). Sometimes people also freeze, like a deer in headlights, which is the third "F" in the fight/flight trio – ever gone silent and dissociated when someone started yelling? That's freeze, an amygdala special. These responses are *automatic*. One minute you were two adults discussing chores; the next, you're basically two startled animals, one possibly roaring and the other metaphorically preparing to play dead or run. As a relationship therapist might say, "When it's hysterical, it's historical" – meaning our over-the-top reactions often come from older, deeper survival wiring. It doesn't excuse bad behavior, but it sure explains why rational communication skills evaporate in the heat of the moment. (In the wise words of every *Star Wars* movie, "Your focus determines your reality" – and if your brain's focus is "danger!", your reality becomes a battlefield.)

The fight-or-flight response in relationships can lead to some comically overblown reactions. Have you ever found yourself in a petty squabble that escalated as if the fate of the world hung in the balance? Like arguing about Netflix choices and suddenly you're both bringing up things from three years ago, voices raised, maybe a vase gets dramatically shattered (*cue telenovela flair*)? That's your hijacked brain talking. One person's primitive defense might be fight mode – yelling, name-calling, getting bigger and louder to "win" (their inner caveman thinks if they dominate, the threat stops). The other person's might be flight – storming out of the room, driving off to cool down, or emotionally shutting off, as if to escape the "attack." Some couples even reenact this dynamic like a script: one pursues, the other distances – a classic anxious vs. avoidant dance, as we saw earlier. It's tragic, but also a little funny, how predictably animalistic we can become. One Psychology Today writer quipped that a partner raising their voice can make the other react "as though they are a slobbering grizzly", with symptoms like panic, hypervigilance, a racing heart and adrenaline surging. *A slobbering grizzly!* Next time you're in an argument, check if your partner has metaphorical fur and claws in your mind's eye – it might explain a lot.

So, how do we get back to our senses? Enter the make-up phase – nature's built-in reconciliation system. Once the initial adrenaline storm passes, our bodies crave a return to equilibrium. This is where those lovely endorphins and oxytocin come in. You know how sometimes after a really intense cry or argument, you feel a strange calm or even euphoria? That's likely endorphins – the body's painkillers – kicking in to soothe you after extreme stress. It's a bit like the runner's high, except you emotionally ran a marathon. And if you and your partner move toward each other (instead of continuing to butt heads), physical affection can be literal medicine. A sincere hug, for instance, can trigger the release of oxytocin, which *lowers* stress and helps rebuild a sense of safety. There's research to back this up: one study found that on days when couples hugged after a conflict, their negative mood was significantly reduced and positive mood increased compared to conflict days with no hugs. Essentially, a warm embrace is telling your body, "You're safe, the threat is gone, this person is actually someone you love." It's like hitting the reset button on that amygdala alarm.

Humorously enough, this makes making up literally the opposite of fight-or-flight: it's tend-and-befriend. You've probably heard of *make-up sex* as a trope – there's some truth to it biologically. After the stress of a fight, all that adrenaline in your system can transmute into passion (the body sometimes mixes up arousal from anger with other kinds of arousal – fun times!). Add a dose of endorphins and oxytocin from physical intimacy, and you both get a calming, bonding high. It's Mother Nature's way of having a couple reaffirm, "We're still in this together," patching up the social bond that the conflict threatened. Of course, you don't *have* to end every fight with bed olympics or even a hug if you're not feeling it – even calm talking and understanding can release oxytocin in a gentler way through feelings of trust and empathy. The key is that once we feel safe again, our parasympathetic nervous system (the "rest and digest" part) can take over, slowing the heart rate and halting the flood of stress hormones. That's why after reconciliation, you might feel physically tired — your body is coming down from a spike of adrenaline and cortisol and shifting into recovery mode.

Let's appreciate the evolutionary comedy here: our ancestors likely developed these intense reactions because choosing the wrong mate or being abandoned had serious survival implications. If Ugg and Ogg argued about how much mammoth meat to share and split up in anger, one might literally die without the other's cooperation. So our bodies treat relationship strife as a five-alarm fire to *prevent* loss of the relationship. Ironically, the very responses meant to protect the bond (yelling to be heard, running to avoid more harm) can damage it in modern times. Thankfully, evolution also gave us big cerebral cortices – the thinking part of the brain – which we can use to *override* these knee-jerk reactions... eventually. That's where communication skills and emotional intelligence come in, helping us step out of the automatic "fight or flight" and instead *talk or hug*. It's not easy in the heat of the moment, but recognizing what's happening in your body can help. Some couples even use safe words or humor as de-escalation tools. For example, one might say, "Honey, my inner cavewoman is about to throw a spear, I need a timeout." A little laughter and meta-awareness can disarm the primal battle and remind both of you that, hey, you're not actually enemies – quite the opposite.

To put it in pop culture terms, a romantic fight can feel like that scene in an action movie where the two heroes, due to a misunderstanding, end up duking it out in an epic battle – until they realize they're on the same side and then team up to defeat the real enemy. In this case, the real enemy is disconnection, or perhaps the pile of wet towels (seriously, just hang them up, it's not that hard!). Remember the movie *Mr. & Mrs. Smith* where Brad Pitt and Angelina Jolie literally beat each other up in their living room, demolishing the house in an ultra-violent confrontation – only to abruptly drop their weapons and make passionate love amidst the rubble? Extreme as that example is (please, no knife fights at home, folks), it captures the pendulum swing of fight and make-up. The intensity of the fight gives way to an equally intense relief and bonding when they realize "I don't actually want to hurt you; I love you." Your nervous system, in less cinematic fashion, is doing the same thing: ramping up for war, then delighting in the peace treaty.

In a more relatable vein, think of a classic sitcom couple known for bickering – say, Lucy and Ricky Ricardo from *I Love Lucy*. They'd get into a spat (Ricky shouting in Spanish, Lucy wailing dramatically), but by the end of the 30 minutes, they'd be in each other's arms, apologizing and laughing. Their faces go from frowns and flushed anger to smiles and maybe a few tears of relief. That warm fuzzy ending part? That's the oxytocin flow, closing the cycle of fight-or-flight and bringing them back to love. Every time a TV couple says "I'm sorry" and hugs it out, a neuroscientist gets their wings (or at least, nods knowingly).

So, what have we learned here in the Love Lab about conflict? Firstly, your crazy physical reactions during a fight (racing heart, shaking, urge to slam a door) are normal – blame your *"slobbering grizzly"* brain for sounding a false alarm. Secondly, understanding this can help you hit pause. When you recognize "Oh, I'm basically in fight-or-flight mode," you can try to slow your breathing, take a break, or do whatever modern tactic works to calm the inner caveperson. Maybe deploy some humor (it's hard to be *too* mad if you imagine your partner as an angry bear or yourself as a hissing cat – it's kind of ridiculous). Finally, making up isn't just a figurative concept; it's a physiological process. A comforting touch, a kind word, a hug or kiss can release the very chemicals that tell your body "Stand down, soldier, all is well." In our conflict resolution toolbox, alongside active listening and "I" statements, we might consider the strategic use of the 20-second hug – as research suggests it can significantly reduce the negative emotional aftershocks of a fight. Science says: Embrace hugging (with consent, of course).

As we end our chapter in the Love Lab, let's circle back to the idea of "science of the heart (and other organs)". It's not just the heart that loves; it's the brain, the adrenal glands, the pituitary pumping out oxytocin, the stomach flipping with butterflies, even the skin craving another's touch. Love is profoundly biological *and* profoundly psychological. We've seen that it can intoxicate us like a drug, bind us together with chemistry akin to superglue, and yes, occasionally drive us up a wall (or up a tree, if you're carving those initials). And yet, knowing all this science doesn't rob love of its mystery – if anything, it makes it more awe-inspiring. How amazing is it that a squishy 3-pound brain can produce sonnets, heartbreak ballads, and midnight cravings to drive across town just for a hug? That the same hormones that helped our ancestors survive emergencies now help us navigate date nights and lovers' quarrels? In the grand experiment of human life, love is perhaps the greatest experiment of all – one we're all a part of, willingly or not.

To quote a pop culture reference with a scientific twist: if love is a lab, we are all its subjects *and* researchers. We stumble, we learn, we laugh (hopefully) at the absurdity of our own reactions. So next time you catch yourself sighing like a Disney character at the sight of your crush, or freaking out as if the sky is falling because your partner forgot an anniversary (again), remember this chapter. Your brain is on love, the chemicals are doing their dance, and you, dear human, are wonderfully normal for riding this rollercoaster. Embrace the science, but don't forget to enjoy the *magic* too – after all, even a lab can be a place of wonder. Now, go give someone a hug (for at least 20 seconds, that's a Love Lab prescription) and let those heartstrings vibrate. Class dismissed – may your hearts be full and your cortisol levels low!

Chapter 10

Happily Ever Aftermath – Embracing the Chaos

Love Lessons 101 (Real Life Edition)

Welcome to Love Lessons 101, real-life edition. No fairy-tale fluff here – just hard-won wisdom from the battlefield of romance. Think of this as the cheat sheet your jaded-yet-wise dating columnist friend would slip you under the table. These tips are scribbled in the margins of *real* life: smudged with pizza grease from date night and highlighted with the neon of hindsight. Here are the messy truths we've learned along the way:

- **Never Ruin an Apology with an Excuse:** A sincere apology is like a unicorn – rare, magical, and *extremely* welcome. If you're sorry, say *sorry*, period. No "I'm sorry you got upset" (that just sneakily blames *them*) and definitely no "I'm sorry, *but…*" which pretty much deletes the apology. Instead, own your actions and acknowledge the impact: e.g. "I'm sorry I forgot our anniversary dinner; I know it hurt your feelings." That kind of apology validates your partner's emotions and opens the door to real dialogue. Pro tip: Do **not** follow it up with, "…but remember that time *you* forgot my birthday?" This isn't a competition (more on that later). The goal is to heal the hurt, not score a point. A genuine, excuse-free apology shows you care more about your partner's feelings than protecting your ego, and that's the stuff of relationship magic. Bonus tip: After apologizing, actually try not to repeat the offense – nothing says "I love you" like *learning* from your mistakes.

- **The Netflix (and Novelty) Compromise:** In modern love, the battle for the TV remote can be as intense as any Shakespearean drama. One of you wants to binge the latest true-crime docuseries while the other desperately needs a rom-com palate cleanser – sound familiar? Learning to compromise on entertainment choices is a surprisingly vital relationship skill. Therapists even say these seemingly trivial TV tiffs are "symbolic, deceptively mundane site[s] of conflict and compromise". In other words, figuring out Stranger Things vs. Bridgerton is really practice for the big stuff. Healthy couples communicate and trade off: maybe tonight is your partner's pick (yes, even if it *is* another three-hour sportsball extravaganza), tomorrow is yours. Some duos develop elaborate systems – from alternating movie choices to the famed "20-minute rule" (if the movie's terrible, you can tap out). The key is remembering you're on the same team. In fact, being willing to grow to like something you initially had zero interest in because your partner loves it is one of the purest forms of love. So next time you find yourself watching a *"dragon show"* (your term for their beloved fantasy series) or they sit through your reality dating trash TV, take heart – this willingness to meet in the middle means your relationship is scoring a win. And hey, you might even discover you enjoy *"the dragon show"* after all.

- **"Calm Down" Is an Invitation to Fireworks:** Quick relationship quiz – when in a heated argument, should you ever tell your angry partner to *"calm down"*? Answer: Only if you actually *want* to witness a Category 5 emotional hurricane. Telling someone on the verge of blowing their top to "calm down" has *never* in the history of love made anyone suddenly serene. On the contrary, anyone who's been on the receiving end of that phrase knows it's gasoline on the fire – dismissive, infuriating, even borderline gaslighting. Experts warn that saying *"Calm down, you're overreacting"* essentially invalidates your partner's feelings and sends the message that *they* are the problem. Pro tip: that's not a message you want to send to the person you love! Instead, let them vent and acknowledge their emotions ("I see you're upset – let's talk about it"). Because telling a fuming person to calm down is like telling a tornado to please take it easy on the trailer park – pointless, and you're likely to get swept up in the next flying cow. If *you're* the one overheated, it's often wiser to pause the argument and cool off rather than say something regrettable. It's perfectly fine to hit the timeout button: as one therapist advises, *"I want to share my feelings, but I need some time to gather my thoughts"*. Take a breather, do some deep breathing, scream into a pillow – whatever works – then come back when you're both more level-headed. Your blood pressure (and your partner) will thank you.

- **Keep Score in Scrabble, Not in Love:** Relationships are not a game to be won, but oh boy, is it tempting to keep score. *I washed* *the dishes, so you should put away the laundry. I apologized first last time, now it's your turn.* Sound familiar? The truth is, keeping a running tally of who did what will drive you both crazy and drive a wedge between you. If you treat your partnership like a spreadsheet of debts and credits, you start seeing your beloved as an opponent rather than a teammate. Healthy couples learn to let go of the quid pro quo mentality. Sure, strive for fairness, but some days one will carry more weight, other days it'll be the other – and that's okay. Maybe they left the toilet seat up (*again*), but hey, you left your wet towel on the bed. Instead of "You always.../You never..." accusations, which shut down communication, try appreciation: notice what your partner *does* do. There's nothing wrong with gently discussing an imbalance (preferably *before* you explode, "Why do I have to do *everything* around here?!"), but do it as a team looking for a solution, not rivals in a blame game. The only place for gloating over victories is board games or fantasy football leagues – in love, you both win or you both lose together. And if you find yourselves arguing over who is more *unfairly* treated, consider this pro tip: swap chores for a day. Walk a mile in each other's shoes (perhaps literally, if one of the chores is walking the dog). It can be eye-opening – and it might just spark a bit of empathy (or at least a laugh when you both realize folding fitted sheets is basically an Olympic sport). Remember, it's you two vs. the problem, not *you vs. each other.* If you insist on keeping score, make it a contest of who can make the other smile more times in a day. Everybody wins that game.

- **Know When to Take a Time-Out:** In kindergarten, time-outs were a bummer. In relationships, time-outs are a *blessing*. We're often taught that if you love someone, you should never go to bed angry or leave an argument unresolved. But real talk: sometimes pressing pause is the best strategy. If a discussion is turning into World War III (or you notice your partner's face doing that scary vein-popping thing), step back before someone says something they can't unsay. As mentioned earlier, it's absolutely fine to say, "I hear you, but I'm too upset to talk calmly. Can we revisit this after a short break?". Taking 20 minutes to walk around the block or an evening to cool off can prevent *weeks* of fallout from a nasty blow-up. The key is to agree on a time to come back and actually address the issue – this isn't sweeping problems under the rug, it's simply preventing a minor issue from turning into a relationship apocalypse. Think of it like this: when your computer freezes, sometimes you need to reboot it. Likewise, a short reboot in a heated moment can return you both to sanity. Just don't use a time-out as a getaway car for avoiding issues entirely; use it as a pit stop, not the finish line. When done right, a cool-off period lets you return to the conversation with cooler heads, clearer thoughts, maybe even a sense of humor about whatever dumb thing you were fighting over. (Trust us, a day later, even the infamous "toilet seat up" incident can start to feel like a scene from a sitcom that you both can smirk about.)

By now, you've probably noticed a theme: the "little" stuff isn't so little. Apologies, TV remotes, tone of voice – these everyday moments are where love either fortifies itself or cracks under pressure. Our Lesson 101 takeaway is that embracing a bit of humility, flexibility, and (when all else fails) strategic silence can turn domestic chaos into an "happily ever aftermath." It's not about avoiding mess – it's about navigating it together with grace, humor, and the occasional perfectly timed "I'm sorry" brownie. Congratulations, class dismissed – you've earned your unofficial PhD in Real-Life Love. Now onto advanced studies in not losing your mind…

Laugh or Cry – Choose Laughter

They say marriage is a comedy to those who think and a tragedy to those who feel. In reality, it's a little of both – but if you get to choose (and you often do), choose laughter. When faced with the absurdities of sharing a life with another human – the miscommunications, the mishaps, the mysteriously multiplying socks – you have two options: laugh or cry. Humor isn't just a bonus in relationships; it's a survival strategy and a secret superglue that binds you together. Science even backs this up: couples who laugh more together tend to have stronger, happier relationships. In one study, lovebirds who burst into shared giggles frequently were more satisfied and felt closer and more supported by their partner than those who kept a straight face. In plainer terms, the couple that laughs together, *lasts* together.

Real-world example: Think of an old married duo cracking up as they recount the disaster of their first date – the one where everything went wrong. Maybe he spilled soup in her lap and then choked on a breadstick; maybe her car died and they ended the night pushing it to a gas station in formal wear. At the time it was mortifying. Now it's their favorite funny story to tell at dinner parties, complete with theatrical reenactments and belly laughs. Shared humor turns your relationship's embarrassing gaffes and everyday failings into inside jokes and fond memories. In fact, researchers have found that how couples reminisce about past events is telling: a classic experiment recorded couples talking about how they first met, and those who were giddy and positive in telling their story were far more likely to stay together in the long run. The pairs who recounted their history with little humor or warmth? More of them ended up in Splitsville. The takeaway: finding the laugh even in life's mishaps is basically relationship insurance.

Humor also defuses tension like a charm. Ever have a fight so ridiculous that one of you just busts out laughing mid-argument? It's *magic* – suddenly the fight evaporates (at least for a moment) and you both remember you're two silly humans who actually like each other. Sure, some issues are no joking matter, but a lot of our day-to-day squabbles are pretty darn absurd when viewed from 10,000 feet. Did we really spend an hour bickering over the "proper" direction of the toilet paper roll? Yes. Yes, we did. (It's over, not under, by the way.) Humor gives perspective. A well-timed goofy face or a playful remark like, "Oh no, we're *that* couple fighting in the grocery aisle – quick, which reality show do you think we'll be cast in?" can break the spell of seriousness. Therapists often encourage couples to cultivate private jokes and lighthearted banter as a way to strengthen bonds. In fact, research out of the University of Kansas spanning 39 studies found that it's not just having a "sense of humor" that matters, but sharing *the same* sense of humor with your partner. It's the unique jokey world that you two create together – those corny pet names, the *"remember when we got lost for two hours because you refused to ask for directions"* anecdotes, even the mutual mockery of each other's weird habits – that forms an intimate bond. When you can both find the same things hysterical, it's like you're speaking a secret language of love… with fart jokes and puns.

And let's not forget the value of *playful* laughter at each other – in the loving way, not the mean way. The happiest couples often gently roast each other, turning personal quirks into affectionate comedy. Take, for example, Hollywood's resident witty couple, Ryan Reynolds and Blake Lively, who famously troll each other on social media for fun. Blake once birthday-posted a photo of Ryan Gosling (wrong Ryan!) and captioned it for her husband, while Ryan Reynolds has posted unflattering pics of Blake or cropped her out as a joke. Their fans eat it up, but more importantly, their humor shows they *get* each other and are secure enough to poke fun. Studies confirm that couples who can playfully tease and make fun of each other (with love!) tend to be very satisfied and secure in their relationship. Playfulness builds trust – if my partner jokes about my terrible singing or your habit of leaving cabinets open, and we both laugh, it tells me I'm loved *with* my flaws (and that maybe my singing really is that bad). As researcher Jeffrey Hall put it, "playfulness between romantic partners is a crucial component in bonding and establishing security". Knowing we can laugh *together* – even when we're laughing at ourselves – makes us feel safe and understood.

So, embrace the goofy side of love. Give each other ridiculous nicknames (yes, Schmoopy Honey Fluff, I'm looking at you). Dance in the kitchen with reckless abandon. Re-watch that stupid comedy you both love for the tenth time. Don't be afraid to unleash your inner dork. Life will supply plenty of reasons to worry or weep; a shared sense of humor is your jointly-owned, renewable supply of joy. As a wise person once said, love is *not* about staring into each other's eyes all the time – it's about both of you staring at the same thing and laughing your butts off. The couples that can find the joke hidden in the chaos are the ones still holding hands 50 years later, chuckling about the fact that one of them still snores like a chainsaw. In the grand rollercoaster of romance, laughter is the safety bar – it keeps you securely together through all the wild twists and turns. Laugh together – it's cheaper than therapy and a lot more fun.

Imperfectly Perfect

Pop quiz: What do sweatpants, morning breath, awkward silences, and snort-laughs have in common? They're all part of the glorious, unglamorous reality of love. Despite what Instagram filters and rom-coms would have us believe, real love is far from perfect – and that's what makes it *perfect*. In fact, one psychologist put it beautifully: *"Real love doesn't thrive in perfection. It lives and breathes in the beautifully messy, unpredictable, and deeply human moments we share with one another."*. Translation: True connection isn't found in the Cinderella moments; it's forged during the 2 a.m. pillow fights, the tear-streaked makeups, and yes, the unsexy

Tuesday nights spent in ratty pajamas debating whose turn it is to order takeout.

We're conditioned to chase the *ideal* partner – the perfectly compatible soulmate who never burps or leaves dirty dishes in the sink. Spoiler alert: that person doesn't exist (and if they did, they'd be *excruciatingly* boring to live with). The sooner we toss out the checklist of "perfect qualities" and embrace the actual quirky human in front of us, the sooner we get to the good stuff. Love means loving someone's *imperfections*, not loving *in spite of* them but *because of* them. The quirky, oddball traits your partner has – maybe they do voices for the cat, or have an annoyingly specific ritual for making coffee – those are the things that make them *them*, and thus endearing. The myth that "happily ever after" involves two flawless people riding off into a sunset is just that: a myth. As one insightful writer quipped, *happily ever after is overrated – true love is about finding someone whose imperfections complement yours, creating a story that's messy, beautiful, and uniquely yours.*

Consider this: You might have once vowed you'd *never* tolerate a partner who leaves socks on the floor. Fast forward and here you are, staring at a rogue sock that your beloved *definitely* left out. Do you (A) start a lecture on cleanliness, or (B) roll your eyes, toss it in the hamper, and affectionately nickname them "Sock Bandit" later? Option B will bring you a lot more peace (and laughs). The point is not to accept genuinely bad behavior or be a doormat – it's to recognize the difference between harmful issues and harmless human quirks. Those little habits and "flaws" are the texture of your life together. They're the inside jokes and the gentle ribbings. Learning to appreciate the unvarnished, un-airbrushed version of your partner is incredibly freeing. Research backs this up: studies show that when partners feel they can be their authentic, imperfect selves, their relationship satisfaction and trust skyrocket. Knowing you don't have to put on a performance of being Mr./Ms. Perfect is such a relief – it creates a "safe space" where both people feel seen and valued for who they *really* are. (Yes, even if who you really are is a person who eats cereal for dinner and wears NASA-themed pajamas – own it, you lovable weirdo.)

Embracing imperfection also means embracing the not-so-glamorous moments. Love isn't just champagne toasts and passionate kisses in the rain. It's also sweatpants date nights where you're curled up on the couch, hair a mess, no makeup, double-dipping chips in the same salsa jar while binging a show that you're half-ashamed to admit you watch. It's the comfort of not having to suck in your gut or mind your Ps and Qs 24/7. It's when your partner has seen you ugly-cry, heard you snore, and knows your weird freckles – and still thinks you're the greatest thing since sliced bread. How powerful is that? To be fully *known* – warts and all – and still fully loved is one of life's greatest feelings. It turns out that even our embarrassing moments can become love-affirming memories. Burning dinner because you got distracted singing into a spatula? Instead of a perfectionist meltdown, the *imperfectly perfect* couple will laugh it off, order pizza, and perhaps crown one another "Chef Disaster 2025" as a joke. And guess what: laughing off a burned meal or a minor mistake like that can actually strengthen your bond by building trust and openness. It sends the signal: "Hey, you don't have to pretend or be perfect for me. I've got you, even when you mess up."

The beauty of embracing each other's imperfections is that it fosters a profound intimacy. When you drop the act and let your partner witness your vulnerable, flawed humanity, you invite them to do the same. Suddenly, a "flaw" isn't a deal-breaker – it's an opportunity to love more deeply. They hate doing laundry but will meticulously detail your car? Great, you can be the Laundry Queen/King and let them handle the car – celebrate the trade-off. He's got a cheesy dad-joke sense of humor that makes *you* groan but the kids love it? Let it roll – someone has to laugh at those puns. Maybe you find her habit of leaving half-full coffee cups around the house exasperating – but also kind of adorable, because it means she's always dreaming and dashing to the next thing. These little things are the threads that weave your shared life. Imperfect moments teach patience, communication, and forgiveness (nothing builds forgiveness like realizing *you* probably have just as many weird habits that need forgiving). Every time you navigate an imperfection with kindness instead of criticism, your relationship grows more resilient. You learn that you can face hiccups together without the sky falling.

So, ditch the airbrushed ideal and revel in the reality. That *real* person beside you – the one with bed-head and a chocolate stain on their shirt, who knows all your weird voices and fears – that person is worth a million fictional Prince Charmings or manic-pixie-dreamgirls. Make peace with the fact that you, too, are gloriously imperfect. And know that in your partner's eyes, those very imperfections might be what make you *irresistibly* lovable. In the end, love is not a Highlights magazine where you circle the differences until you "fix" them; love is more like a Jackson Pollock painting – a beautiful mess. Up close it's splatters and chaos, but step back and you'll see the masterpiece. Perfect is boring; imperfect together is an adventure.

The Thrill and the Agony

After all this talk of chaos – the fights over TV shows, the tears and the laughs, the socks on the floor and the toothpaste cap left off – a reasonable person might ask: why on earth do we put ourselves through this? Love, frankly, can be a pain in the butt. It's certainly *inconvenient* (news flash: sharing a bathroom is never fairy-tale elegant). It's often maddening. And yet… nearly all of us are drawn to love like moths to a flame. Are we all just masochists, or is there some method to this madness?

The answer, dear reader, is both simpler and deeper: we pursue love because the *highs* are sky-high, and even the lows give meaning to our lives. The thrill and the agony are two sides of the same coin – you can't fully have one without the other. Yes, love will, at times, drive you up the wall. But it will also give you moments of transcendent joy that make the whole rollercoaster ride worthwhile. Think about that feeling of pure bliss the first time you realized you were in love – the racing heart, the goofy grin you couldn't wipe off your face. Or the comfort of coming home on a terrible day to a hug that makes all the bad stuff melt for a moment. The thrill of love can be as dramatic as a grand proposal on a mountaintop, or as simple as sharing a quiet cup of coffee on a Sunday morning with someone who truly gets you. Those little moments of connection – laughing at a dumb joke together, getting a spontaneous shoulder squeeze when you're stressed, even companionable silence as you both scroll on your phones under a cozy blanket – they add up to something truly profound: a life less lonely, a heart more full.

And guess what? Beyond the poetic stuff, there are science-backed benefits to this whole love business (as if we needed more convincing). Decades of research have shown that people in healthy relationships *literally* live healthier, longer lives. For instance, being married or in a committed partnership is associated with lower rates of heart attacks, a stronger immune system, and even living longer than singles on average. One large study found that married folks tended to live longer and were less likely to die of certain causes like heart disease or even accidents – perhaps because having someone who cares whether you come home at night subconsciously makes you take fewer stupid risks (no guarantees though; couples can do plenty of stupid things *together*, but I digress). Additionally, those in supportive relationships often have lower stress levels – researchers note that the happily partnered have lower cortisol (stress hormone) levels and better blood pressure than their unhappily or un-partnered peers. Emotional support literally calms your nervous system. Knowing there's someone in your corner – whether it's to vent about your awful boss or to bring you ginger ale when you've got the flu – can make life's pressures feel manageable. As one social worker put it, *having people you can rely on encourages healthy habits, reduces stress, and provides emotional support, all of which contribute to a longer, healthier life.* In short, love might drive you crazy, but it also keeps you sane. Go figure!

Love has other perks: people in love tend to recover faster from illness, experience less depression, and even report higher life satisfaction. There's even research showing that being in a stable, loving relationship can *literally* reduce pain – holding your partner's hand can ease physical pain in stressful situations, as if the body knows "I'm not alone in this" and turns down the pain dial. Heck, love can even help you sleep better – happily married couples are 10% more likely to get a good night's sleep, probably because it's easier to rest when there's a trusted human spooning you (even if they occasionally snore directly in your ear). It's as if we're biologically wired to thrive with a partner by our side.

But beyond the health stats and longevity charts lies something less tangible but just as crucial: the existential joy of being known and accepted by another human being. In a world where we're all a little lonely and constantly pressured to put on a perfect front, having that one person who sees your whole messy self and says "I'm here for it – I'm here for *you*" is nothing short of miraculous. We chase love because deep down, we all long for that acceptance. To find a partner in crime who looks at our collection of nerdy video games or hears about our childhood traumas and doesn't run away – instead, they lean in and say, "Tell me more." That feeling is incomparable. Love lets us experience being truly *seen*. And when someone truly sees you and still sticks around to binge-watch an entire season of The Office with you while you're wearing zit cream and eating cold pizza – that's something holy right there.

Let's not forget the *fun* of it all, too. Love is an adventure, the ultimate choose-your-own-romantic-comedy. The emotional highs – the butterflies of a first kiss, the goofy excitement of dancing in the kitchen, the pride that swells when you see your partner shine at something they love – those highs are higher than almost anything else life offers. Sure, the lows can be pretty low (heartbreak and disappointment are part of the package, unfortunately). But as Tennyson famously said, *'Tis better to have loved and lost than never to have loved at all.* Corny? Maybe. True? Absolutely. Even the agony teaches us, shapes us, and reminds us that we're alive and connected.

In the big picture, love is one of the fundamental ways we find meaning. We might laugh now about who left the toilet seat up or who forgot to hit the trash takeout day, but when life hits us with real challenges – a loss, a scare, a dream on the line – it's our partner's hand we squeeze, their shoulder we lean on. The shared life we build, messy and chaotic as it is, becomes a shelter in the storm. And in the quiet mundane moments, there's a profound contentment in companionship. As humans, we're wired for connection; love is the ultimate connection. It's why we keep downloading the dating apps, why we risk vulnerability, why we say "I do" and start families and merge Netflix accounts. Love, with all its madness, gives us stories to tell, memories to treasure, and someone to share the popcorn with during the movie of life.

So yes, love can make you want to pull your hair out. It's chaos, it's compromise, it's occasionally wondering if your partner was put on this earth specifically to annoy you. But it's also staring at the ceiling at 3 a.m., laughing uncontrollably about an inside joke no one else would get. It's feeling the weight of the world lift because they whispered "It's going to be okay, we've got this." It's knowing that in a universe of 8 billion people, you've found one who is your home. That's the thrill *and* the agony of love – and we embrace the chaos because the reward is nothing less than everything. Despite the madness, despite the mess, we keep falling in love, staying in love, fighting and forgiving and figuring it out. Because at the end of the day, a life without the crazy, beautiful, gut-wrenching, hilarious truth of love would be a far poorer life indeed. Happily ever after isn't a neat ending – it's the daily choice to love and laugh through whatever life throws at you, together. And that, dear reader, is why it's all worth it. Here's to embracing the chaos – and finding our own perfect amidst the imperfection, our own happily in the ever *aftermath*.

Epilogue

So here we are, dear beloved, having survived page after page of romantic carnage, domestic warfare, and the eternal mystery of bathroom etiquette.

The truth is, love makes liars of us all. We lie about our past, our weight, our browser history, and yes, our role in the Great Toilet Seat Conspiracy of every relationship since indoor plumbing was invented. We confess to things we didn't do and hide things we absolutely did. We regret the chances we took and the chances we didn't, sometimes simultaneously while standing in line at Target.

But here's the beautiful paradox: in all our messy, contradictory, pants-around-our-ankles humanity, we keep trying. We keep falling in love, leaving toilet seats in compromising positions, and believing that maybe—just maybe—this time we'll get it right. And sometimes, gloriously, we actually do. If you believe that, can you shout an AMEN!!!

www.ingramcontent.com/pod-product-compliance
Lightning Source LLC
Chambersburg PA
CBHW061747120626
46550CB00005B/1912